SPIRITUALITY AND THE GENTLE LIFE

By

ADRIAN VAN KAAM, C.S.Sp.

DIMENSION BOOKS, INC.

Denville, New Jersey

1974

Published by Dimension Books, Inc.
Denville, New Jersey 07834

Imprimi Potest: *Rev. Philip J. Haggerty, C.S.Sp.*
Provincial

Nihil Obstat: *Rev. William J. Winter, S.T.D.*
Censor Librorum

Imprimatur: *Most Rev. Vincent M. Leonard, D.D.*
Bishop of Pittsburgh

June 24, 1974

CONTENTS

FOREWORD

This book presents a collection of meditative reflections on the theme of spirituality and gentleness.

While it may be advantageous to follow the sequence of chapters and prayers as presented, this is by no means necessary for fruitful understanding. A reader may select at random a chapter or prayer that appeals more immediately to his present needs and aspirations. The main thing in spiritual reading of this kind is to slow down, to relax, to allow oneself ample time to dwell meditatively on the chapter or prayer one has chosen; and to return to it prayerfully whenever the need arises.

It is my pleasant duty to thank Rev. Bert van Croonenburg, C.S.Sp., S.T.D. and Dr. Susan Muto Ph.D., respectively executive director and assistant director of the Center for the Study of Spirituality, for their invaluable suggestions which considerably influenced the content and expression of this book.

I am grateful also to Sr. Margaret Gall, S.D.R., publication manager of the Center, who generously typed the final manuscript and to Sr. Dorothy Majewski, C.S.F.N., Secretary, who patiently assisted in laborious proof reading and other details of readying the manuscript for publisher and printer.

Pittsburgh, May 12, 1974,

Adrian van Kaam, C.S.Sp.

Director of the Center for the Study of Spirituality, Institute of Man Duquesne University.

PART ONE

THE GENTLE LIFE STYLE

I

SPIRITUAL APPROACH TO GENTILITY

Spiritual life may be most simply defined as the art and discipline of presence to the Sacred. To make it easier for me to be faithful to this life, I must foster certain virtues that facilitate living in the Divine Presence.

Human virtues are not enough; they must be transformed by grace. Yet this gift of grace does not diminish the demands made upon me. Grace keeps asking me to grow humanly and spiritually. This does not mean that I should make the development of virtue the last aim of my life. I might then fall into a kind of idolatry, making human perfection my god. I might, in other words, close myself off from the radiance of divine grace and bury myself in the pursuit of a merely human perfection. If this happens, I should try to become aware of it, humble myself, and admit that I am after all a fallen human being. Humbling myself before Him at the height of arrogance helps overcome the tendency to be my own savior. I am in touch once again with the divine power of restoration. I yield to Him; He yields to me. I drink from the stream of living waters.

The other extreme would be to over-react to the danger of a mere humanism. Then I might become excessively fearful of anything natural and spontaneous in myself—fearful of the human meaning and value of my attitudes. I move from one extreme to the other. First, I was one-sidedly taken in by the role I myself played in the unfolding of my life. Now I may be fascinated as one-sidedly by the role of God in my sanctification. This new extreme is as destructive to real growth as the former exaggeration. I am tempted to cancel out as a freely cooperating person in the vain expectation that everything will be achieved by grace alone. I neglect to develop facilitating human conditions for a life lived in the light of His grace. I look with suspicion upon the human side of graced attitudes. I forget that the Holy Trinity dwells in my human soul, incarnated in psyche and body.

The unfolding of my graced life takes into account human virtues that evolve daily in my interaction with myself, with fellow men, and with my life situation. I should not see my sanctification as a divine event in which I have no place and play no role. I should not dream that the castle of the Holy floats above me, beyond daily life, when actually it is a castle at the heart of my human existence.

Gentleness is one of the attitudes that can facilitate my presence to Father, Son and Spirit. This attitude

too has to be permeated by grace. Also here I should
be aware of its human dimension.

Gentleness transformed by divine grace is the royal
road to Divine Presence. A mere human way to God
would prove to be a dead-end street. Because we are
fallen men, gentleness cannot reach perfection outside the realm of grace and the redeeming love of
Jesus.

In spirituality we are concerned not only with
thinking about attitudes like gentleness but with
living them. Not thought but life is our center of
interest. In spirituality we want to understand all
things from the viewpoint of daily life, taking into
account faithfully the fundamental doctrine of the
Church. We seek for an understanding that serves a
deepening of our life with God.

Many people have thought about gentle behavior as
it relates to social effectiveness; to the development
of a gentleman as influenced by his environment; to
what role gentleness plays in diverse cultures and
religions. All of these questions are interesting and
necessary. The answer to them is important for our
understanding of man's development in and through
society. But the same questions and answers do not
suffice for our inner spiritual growth nor our understanding of it. We are not so much interested in the
way man relates outwardly to society; our interest
centers rather on the inner truth and value of the
attitudes we display in our social life.

A person who is a perfect gentleman in the social
sense may not be a gentle man at all spiritually. He

may not have cultivated the true virtue of gentleness, only the outer mask. During certain cultural periods whole generations may only play at being gentlemen. Their gentleness may be no more than an outward imitation of gentile manners that characterize the socially privileged. A surface gentility like that would be useless for growth in sanctity. In no way would it ready man for the experience of the indwelling of the Divine in self, others, and nature.

Some people may suspect an inner emptiness behind outer gentility. This feeling may explain the scornful way they react to the smooth behavior of the accomplished gentleman. They may not really trust him. Something about him makes them cautious lest they be taken in. In many cases their suspicion is unjustified, but on occasion their intuition seems to be right. Gentleness is so attractive and winning a quality, soothing for body and soul, that a clever man of the world, who despises gentleness deep down, may still imitate its outward manifestation. He may feign its appearance to further his self-centered aims.

Social abuse of the gentle life style makes it even more mandatory for spirituality to search for the inner meaning of gentleness as it reveals itself in daily life. Look at the simple and familiar everyday expressions of gentleness—the understanding smile, the comforting handshake, the delicate use of sympathetic words. Such simple manifestations of gentleness can be a departure for spiritual reflection. In them gentility expresses itself in a most tangible way.

The inwardness of gentility is manifested in patient meditative reflection on a beneficient look, a respectful silence, an understanding smile, a careful choice of words and gestures to avoid hurting a person, a compassionate acceptance of our own failures, an inner experience of mellowing anger in certain situations.

To know gentility we have to probe the deeper meaning of such simple gestures and experiences whose significance we rarely follow through in thought and life. We don't think them through *because* they are familiar. Our very familiarity with them makes us take them for granted. What is most near to us seems most to resist our reflection.

In this book we shall reflect spiritually on those special aspects of love and charity that are indicated by the word gentleness. We will look thoughtfully at daily experiences of gentleness, especially gentleness towards ourselves. Spiritual reflection on manifestations of gentleness in a variety of situations may help us to understand the inner spiritual meaning of human gentleness and its role in the spiritual emergence of man.

It is difficult, however, to really understand the living truth of gentleness if I am not experiencing gentleness and its obstacles in my own life. I can only begin to grasp the experiental meaning of gentleness when I myself have tried to be gentle. I need not have the experience of a perfect gentleness that would pervade my whole being. It is sufficient for my reflection that I am on the way to gentleness.

When I honestly try to be gentle, I am bound at some moment to experience this virtue. At many more moments I will experience obstacles to gentleness. They too can give me insight into the gentle life style and the dynamics of its unfolding. They do so by way of contrast. Experiences of failure are like the negative of a photo. By showing what true gentility is not, they show me indirectly what the real thing may be. I cannot have the benefit of such negative experiences if I am not on the way. I can only be aware of losing my way when I have tried to find and follow it in the first place. I should thus try to walk the way of gentility, no matter how awkwardly. Once I begin to live and reflect upon my own limited experiences of gentleness I can complement these with the experiences of others.

Our aim is thus to understand how we may better live and experience human gentleness, culminating in a graced gentle presence to God, ourselves, and others.

II

SPIRITUALITY AND GENTILITY

The word gentleness does not point to a thing like a stone in my shoe or a signpost along the road. It points to an attitude. One way to search for the meaning of words that refer not to things but to attitudes is to look for the adjective included in the noun, in our case the noun "gentleness." The adjective "gentle" may help me to look at the ways in which the noun is used to describe people, things, events or actions.

For example, I can say: a gentle word, a gentle kiss, a gentle gesture, a gentle feeling, a gentle approach. I do not say: a gentle stone, a gentle bridge, a gentle thunder, a gentle blow, a gentle war.

In the first series of examples, I notice that the word gentle points to the expressions, attitudes, and behavior of human beings.

Is it not also true that a certain behavior of animals makes us think about gentleness? Young colts are licked by their mother. Perhaps we can also speak here about gentleness. Animals are similar to us in many ways and yet different. We feel inclined to ascribe to animals expressions of gentleness because their behavior makes us think about our behavior.

Expressions like a gentle gesture, a gentle word, a gentle approach, are all said of human behavior that expresses certain inner feelings or attitudes.

One can also speak about a "gentleman." Think about the English word. It seems to indicate that gentleness can become a characteristic of a person as a whole and not merely of some of his expressions. Gentleness can become a lasting attitude, affecting or transforming one's personality. Gentleness directs itself to something or someone in a distinctive way; it implies a special relation of a person to God, to himself, to others, to things.

What is it that evokes this gentleness? Gentleness is usually enkindled by something that is precious but vulnerable. Everything that appears fragile and vulnerable and at the same time precious in some way seems to evoke gentleness: a sick person, a child, a pregnant woman, the victim of an accident. All that is small and somehow precious: a baby, a newborn puppy, an old woman emaciated by age and sickness. Yet also something large and powerful can evoke gentleness. A person could feel gentle about the boss of a large company who is all bluster and no bite. Gentleness is not evoked by the impressive function and power of the boss but by the vulnerability of inner endearing traits that hide behind a facade of strength.

Greatness evokes gentleness in so far as it refers to the vulnerability of hidden precious qualities that one knows to be a deeper characteristic of the person. In that sense Christ, and later the apostles, speak often about the faithful as children, no matter how tall, rich, clever and successful they may be. For behind each one's strength is hiding a fallen person in need of redemption, a person precious in the eyes of God because of the unique treasure he is meant to be in time and eternity.

We may not feel gentle towards God the Almighty Father when meditating on His transcendent Divine Power. What we feel is reverence, adoration, awe A gentle feeling can be evoked however by God, made vulnerable in the child at Bethlehem or in the man of suffering in the garden or on the cross.

All that is pure, unblemished, and immaculate can also evoke feelings of gentleness because its exquisiteness seems so fragile and open to contamination: the bright wonder of an idealistic young man, the innocent questions of a child, the unsuspecting spontaneity of an adolescent girl, make us gentle in our approach to them.

Finally, all that is beautiful can make us gentle for we feel that it can be marred so easily: the perfection of a painting, the radiance of a human face, the attractiveness of a fresh flower. In these and many more ways beauty touches us and evokes gentleness.

The last examples show that I can feel gentle about things. I would not be moved to gentleness by a pile of rubbish, a heap of sand, a mound of earth. I may feel gentle, however, whenever this mound of earth covers the grave of someone I love. If the wind blows scraps of paper on this earth, I bend over gently and remove them with care. If an animal leaves its footprints there, I wipe them out gently. Clearly this mound of earth makes me feel more gentle, but only because it tells me about the beloved person buried there.

We may thus treat things gently because they are fragile and precious like a painting or a flower. They may be precious in themselves or they may be precious because of the love or the beloved they symbolize. A mother may treasure the first awkward drawing her little Johnny made for her. She treats this fragile piece of paper gently as something precious because it symbolizes for her the loveliness of her child.

For some deeply spiritual people all creatures are suffused by divine love. Every creature may evoke in them a loving gentility. The more they become spiritual, the more the world lights up for them as a symbol of the Holy Presence. This graced vision transforms their life style. A delicate gentleness of gesture, word, and manner begins to pervade their lives. One is struck by their gentle approach not only to people but to the simplest things they handle. They seem to sense that all things are mirrors of divine love and beauty. They are tender and fragile; they can be abused and broken; their modest reflection of eternal splendor may be easily dimmed.

A person who attends a meal of Buddhist monks is moved by the recollected and respectful gentleness with which they handle their chopsticks and the food given to them. Later, when you see the monks laboring in the garden, you are struck by the same respectful use of tools, by their gentle tending of flowers, small rock gardens, plants and shrubbery.

Awareness of the presence of the Divine instills gentleness in the human soul. This same gentleness seems in turn to deepen awareness of the Presence that evoked this feeling in the first place. The key to a gentle life style, that pervades all thoughts, feelings and actions, seems to be a continuous awareness of the Divine Presence.

Can I be gentle with myself? From what we have uncovered thus far about gentleness, I can be gentle with myself if I can experience myself simultaneously as precious, fragile and vulnerable. I know from daily experience that I am not always faithful to my precious divine life call. Many times I feel disappointed in myself, experiencing how I prevent my better self from flourishing. In fact, I am often my greatest disappointment. Most people are not inclined to feel gentle towards this disappointing self because they do not look with love at the precious person God calls them to be. They either feel indifferent or they refuse to see their shortcomings and limitations. When they begin to see how fragile and vulnerable their precious selfhood is, they feel either frustrated, desperate or angry with themselves. Such self-condemnation does not give rise to a gentle approach to the divine treasure of their true graced self. At such moments I want to whip myself into shape. I feel that I have to discipline myself mercilessly, forgetting that I may harm my finer sensitivities and silence the whisper of the Spirit within my heart.

What is that other self that reproaches me so unkindly? It is the voice of my pride and anxious concern to look good in my own eyes and in the eyes of others. I do not accept the limited but precious person I can be. I ask myself only what others may think about me, how I can get ahead in society, even at the expense of the unique potential excellence God calls me to. I cannot forgive myself when I don't live up to the standards a competing community sets for me. Such alien standards may have been inculcated in me when I was a child. My parents may have forced upon me many do's and don'ts that would assure me success in the eyes of family, neighbors, school, and church.

Even from this short look, it should be clear that I can experience myself as simultaneously precious, fragile and vulnerable and therefore develop an attitude of gentleness towards myself. Many people see themselves only as bad, undisciplined, lazy and willfully resisting improvement. There is undoubtedly some truth in all this. But it is not the whole truth. If there is sometimes bad will in me, lack of discipline, and laziness, it is due partly to a deeper weakness in my make-up that hinders the unfolding of the unique eminence God calls me to.

A first step to inner gentleness is thus to gratefully love myself as a unique divine gift and to admit and accept my weakness which makes me the fragile earthen vessel of this treasure. As long as I pretend that I am strong, that I by myself can live up to the unique eminence God calls me to in Christ, I cannot be gentle with myself. Gentleness with self is possible only when I recognize and "own" also the vulnerability of the treasure I am. I must be able to look at myself with a forgiving eye. This may seem almost impossible because there is something in me that tells me that I cannot forgive myself.

I am responsible to something or someone infinitely greater than I. Here again I meet the mystery of Divine Presence. It is neither society nor my ego that can ultimately forgive me but the Divine Ground from which I emerge, that makes me be, and allows me in the experience of forgiveness to rediscover the divine gift of my unique eminence in spite of my unfaithfulness. My self-presence must share in His forgiving presence to me. My fragile life, like the life of all other creatures, is suffused by His presence which is a call to be lovingly loyal to my graced uniqueness. To be aware of God's presence helps me to approach my fragile best self gently and kindly.

In the course of our meditative reflections on gentleness, we shall see how this gentleness toward my fragile precious self as called forth uniquely by God constitutes the core of gentleness with others and with the manifold created appearances of the

Divine in my surroundings, how it is also a main condition for my presence to God.

Most fragile is my presence to the Divine Presence; only grace can maintain it. The gift of presence implies the gift of gentleness. Awareness of the Divine is subtle and sublime, of such fragility and finesse that it may disappear the moment my willfulness and pride take over and try to force the felt presence of this Infinite Guest. Silent cooperation with the divine gift of gentility can thus keep at bay any arrogant movement on the part of my fallen soul that might chase away the loving presence of the Holy.

Lord,
The earth lights up
As a symbol
Of your presence;
All nature is suffused
With your light and life.
Let everything of beauty
Evoke in me
Loving gentility:
Each one is a reflection
Of your eternal splendor,
Each one a mirror
Easily dimmed
If I don't tend it
With gentility.
Let the awareness
Of your presence
Instill gentleness
In my soul;
Gentleness towards myself too,
The broken mirror of your love.
Let my self-presence share
In your forgiving presence
Of my fragile life.

III

THE GENTLE LIFE STYLE

I spent part of last summer writing a paper. My decisiveness to get the thing over and done with made me feel tense and strained. Before going any further, I began to tell myself, "This time try to do your work with ease of mind." So I tried. I began to muse in a leisurely way about my topic. I read thoughtfully material related to it. Only then did I feel ready to write out a few paragraphs or pages. When the work became too much, I would stroll in a nearby park, look at the flowers, follow the antics of playful ducks in the pond. I tried not to let myself become upset, strained or willful. Neither did I try to obtain the results of my study instantly. I was sure my topic would speak to me in its own good time if I would keep myself quietly open for hints, sudden associations, flashes of insight. My faithful readings and reflections would sooner or later show me the main aspects of the question I was dealing with.

So I trusted. I also kept my inner freedom to occasionally close my books, halt my typing, and leave my notes to enjoy the radiance of the sun in the garden or the pleasant breeze along the lanes and meadows of the park. My new way worked. Slowly I could feel the ideas rise, the right words come. A gentle perseverance in my attention to the topic and its expression proved sufficient for the paper to be written.

At first I had approached my task with the anxious drive to get the work over with. Now I had given myself over to the calming effect of a gentle life style. I could almost feel the tautness leaving my head, the tenseness draining from my muscles. No longer was the will to force things present in me. I did not command my topic to make itself clear at once. I was content to be nothing more than I could be at the moment, content to make as much headway as I was humanly able to. There was no compulsion to be more efficient, more clever or faster than I reasonably could be in a relaxed manner. Gone was the eagerness to hurry up the process of production. The spirit of gentility had invaded my work.

On other occasions my feelings were quite the opposite. At such times I wanted desperately to gain time. I came to my writing with a vehemence that shut out anything my topic itself could give to me when patiently waited upon. The work had to be done as fast as possible I felt, and the topic itself was not going to play a part in its production. I did not give the topic much chance to show itself to me. I ran through books and articles without really allowing them to affect me. The topic spoke but I could not hear its message because I did not approach it gently, as a reflective person should. My readings contained hints and suggestions, but I as a gentle receptive listener was not there to receive them. Many pages were pregnant with meaning but not for me. Instead I gathered surface information as fast as I could. No time was given to let it sink in, to make it part of myself, to recreate it in my own manner.

For the process of thought and its precise expression, time is of the essence. Gentility allows time to run its course. My concern was to gain time. I typed my information out like a reporter on the city desk. While I was hurrying on, I was concerned neither with the kind of people who would read my paper nor with the people around me and their needs.

By contrast, gentility opens me to what people, events, and things may disclose to me or reasonably want of me. I allow these persons and things to change and affect me when such change is called for. Gentleness is an attitude of letting be, combined with a patient abiding with myself or with the person, task, or problem God calls me to be involved in. This attitude leads to peace and contentment.

I can be busily engaged in a demanding task like writing a paper, organizing a business deal, fighting for a cause and yet be gentle inwardly. One condition is to keep in tune with the real me and with my real life situation and not to become a prisoner of my projects or of the outcome of my task. It is unrealistic to strive after something I cannot reach without overextending myself. Such efforts wear me out. I feel frustrated when I cannot reach goals too sublime for me. Even when I achieve such goals, frustration may still result. I may have so depleted myself by vehement strife that I cannot enjoy my success. It may seem meager in comparison to all I had to go through to make this achievement come true. For too long a time I may have used my life as merely a tool for achievement in the eyes of others. In spite of momentary success, I suffer the frustration of a vehement or willful life.

In contrast, the gentle attitude leaves room for what is more than mere usefulness. When I am willful instead of gentle, I program my life. Things are not allowed to appear to me as they are. The willful man squeezes every experience in a tight little box tied up with unbreakable strings. His mind becomes a store house of these little air tight compartments. He does not allow any new situation to touch the content of his store. What he has done is to forfeit his ability to abide with things as if for the first time. He moves through life as a programmed computer lacking any sense of wonder.

A vehement or willful person cannot "let go" in prayer, love, or play. The most relaxing activity becomes just another form of work for him. He brings to love or play the same demands for accomplishment that deaden his daily life. Soon his spirit dies too.

The gentle person is more free. He can take himself and the world as they are because he feels free to be himself and to let all things be with the same gentility. There is a friendly accord between him and his life situation. He does not feel that he has to push himself forward or hold himself back. At home with himself he approaches every task and event in gentle self-possession. If he cannot feel at ease with what he is doing, he can put it aside for another time when he can more readily give his all. If the situation demands that he go on with the work at hand—in spite of his reluctance—he gently does what cannot be delayed. He does not allow himself to become upset by the less perfect outcome due to the inauspiciousness of the moment. He takes things in stride. Being a gentle man he never forces people or situations. Neither would he tolerate anyone who forces himself or others, were he able to ward off such imposition. All people, events, and things, no matter how insignificant, draw his respect, for they all emerge from the same mystery. The motto of the gentle man might well be, "I must never force things."

In living the gentle life style, I may discover something else. It becomes easier for me to pray, to meditate, to stay attuned to God's presence. Gentility stills and quiets the greediness and aggressiveness of the ego. A silenced ego allows me to center myself in my divine ground. While it is helpful to have a strong ego, it is harmful to center my life in that ego alone. Greediness and arrogance might then absorb all of my life. I would be so busy keeping my ego sublime, sane, and successful that no time would be left for a gentle nursing of my soul in the light of God's gentility.

Any true gentility, human or divine, mellows the ego, not by weakening its strength but by diminishing its arrogance, its false exclusiveness, its pretense of ultimacy. Any diminishment of the ego's arrogance makes me more available to the Divine.

The asceticism of the gentle life style is already a path to God's presence. Once I live in that presence my gentility may deepen and gain a quality it could never obtain by asceticism alone. It is deepened by a divine gift; it becomes a peace that passes understanding, a peace the world cannot give. Because it is a gift, I must ask God to grant it to me. My very beseeching will remind me that evangelical gentility is His gift, not my doing. This reminder is important. For I may forget my dependence on the Divine during my self-preparation for this that complements and transforms my human gentility. God wants me to do what is humanly possible to grow daily in gentility. My effort shows my good will, my increasing readiness for His gift of gentility, when it comes to me in His own good time.

My human attempt to live the gentle life is my promise of cooperation with the grace of gentility once it touches my life. The human attempt to grow in gentility is necessary, yet it may tempt me to forget that its outcome is only provisional, a shadow of things to come—the real thing being the divine gentleness of soul that is a pure gift of the Holy.

SPIRITUALITY AND THE GENTLE LIFE

Lord,
You want me to learn from you
Gentleness of heart.
No matter how I fail you,
Your gentleness never fails me.
You are slow to anger;
Your kindness is without limit.
You tell me not to be distressed,
To make your gentleness my own
So that my soul may find rest.
Give me the wisdom to make time in my day
For a gentle nursing of my soul.
Free me from arrogance,
From goals too sublime for me.
Still and quiet my soul
As a mother quiets the little ones on her lap.
Free me from the need for achievement.
Make my life less forceful, more gentle,
Centered in you alone.
Let the splendor of your presence
Light up my everydayness.
Make me a smooth channel for the outflow
Of your Divine Will in this world.
Let me move gently
In the omnipresence of the Divine.
Harmonize my frail spirit with the Infinite Spirit
Who fills the universe and its history.
Love of my Lord,
Invade my soul and melt away any trace of vehemence.

IV

LISTENING AND THE GENTLE LIFE

When I am gentle, I have time to listen. I have time to be quiet, to think without strain, to work without pressure. There is time to look at birds and flowers and blooming trees. Time to enjoy music, to see friends, to laugh and talk, to be silent and alone. Above all, there is time to pray, time for many moments of prayerful presence to the Divine. Gentleness finds time to listen to the goodness and truth of the persons and things I meet and time for presence to the Divine Origin that is in and beyond them.

Instead of being gentle, I may be impassioned or vehement, grim or tough, willful or strained. Then my listening is impaired. Time becomes so pressing that it begins to possess me. I am no longer available to the mystery of Divine Presence that may light up in every event and thing for those who have time to listen. I feel that I must cram every moment with something useful or exciting. I cannot afford the refreshment of a recreative pause during my hours of performance. I cannot sit still, distancing myself for some moments from the pressure of my daily concerns. Such a life makes prayer impossible, for life ceases to be a preparation for the precious moments of listening to the Divine.

To be sure, I have other stands to take. I have to be at times concerned, strong, aggressive. Such stands in and by themselves do not make me ready or unready for the life of prayer. What matters is how I live such attitudes. Have they become so exclusive in my life that gentleness wholly disappears and in no way lingers on in the background of my existence ready to emerge when the time is ripe? While living up concretely to the sometimes harsh demands of daily life, do I find sufficient nourishment for my inward gentleness so as not to succumb to the necessary pragmatic and aggressive roads I have to walk repeatedly?

With such nourishment, I can keep my life open for God without becoming soft and powerless in daily endeavors. I take life gently as it comes. Gentle acceptance of life from the hand of God implies at times the acceptance of strong stands and courageous approaches, but the deeper acceptance at the root of all of them is based on an all pervasive gentleness and receptivity. To keep awake the power of listening to the beyond in daily life is to keep alive the power of presence.

When I take life gently as it comes, I find that I can sit and listen to a friend without talking, share the play of a child without interfering, console a fellow man without being obtrusive. When I am gentle, communication with the Divine becomes communion.

Many of us long for such gentleness in ourselves and others. It is like a treasure lost, buried under the pressures of an achievement society. Gentleness clearly does not exclude strong and courageous stands. I can rest or work, give in to people or fight with them, both gently and violently. Gentleness is more than relaxation and giving in; it is more than the opposite of fight, work, ambition. It is an attitude which affects and changes the style of my play or work, my fight or surrender, my admiration or rightful indignation. How I fight, argue, study, entertain, work or play then reveals the presence or absence of gentleness in my life.

The difference between a gentle and vehement response to my task in this world lies in the stand I take. I may work in a gentle mood, allowing myself to be open to everything that touches significantly upon what I am doing. The web of persons, events, places, and things with which my task is interwoven may change daily. This makes my daily task a new happening in some respects. If gentle, I do not resent such continual change but listen to it as the ongoing self-disclosure of a Divine Will incarnating itself each day of my life.

When I am willful instead of gentle, I try to program my life. I impose my own will and meaning on the world. Gentleness, on the other hand, helps me to hear in each new situation subtle nuances that emerge because of slight changes in the people and circumstances connected with it. The orderly managing me does not want to be upset by such changes. They interfere with the neatness of my project. They break up the flow of my practical pursuits. When gentle, I listen to the situation as God allows it to be. I flow with it obediently. I quietly give myself over to it. Wedded to it in this way, I am not preoccupied with countless other things to be experienced or done later. I am at one with the tools I hold, the things I touch, the persons I talk to, with the matter I explain or show to people. In and through them, I am at one with the Divine Will which speaks in all of them.

To see life gently means more than seeing it with a calculating eye or listening to it with a willful ear. The gentle look sees life beyond the work-a-day meaning it also has. A gentle listening to the world gives me the opportunity to hear its revelation anew. Without gentleness, I may see and hear my surroundings only as a place of duty, strife, survival. My work becomes merely an occasion to make money, to overcome boredom, to further my career. When this harsh stance takes over, I lose the gentle vision of life that may have been mine as a child. My heart hardens. My eyes are blinded. My ears no longer hear. I no longer perceive the glory of God in the place where I live and in the work I do.

Gentleness sets me free from such a suffocating stance. People, events, and things begin to nourish my spiritual life. They lift my heart to God. They disclose a Divine Presence to be adored in and beyond the necessary nitty-gritty of daily performance.

Gentleness is a special way of listening to myself and others and all that happens in my life. The gentle attitude draws me out in a whole new way. My views of life may have been colored by my need to cast the world in my own image instead of in the image of the Divine. I may have been dominated by a need to keep others at bay or to push ahead of them ruthlessly. I could not listen to the Divine Presence in my situation. Therefore, I did not allow events and things to speak their own meanings to me, apart from my plans for them. I could not hear or see them in the perspective of the Eternal.

Gentleness becomes possible when my surroundings are cast in a divine light. The gentle attitude, nourished by my presence to the Divine, takes me out of the world of willfulness. It turns me into a new person who sees and hears and moves in the light of the Sacred, whose Divine Gentleness bathes all in its wake.

Gentleness makes me more aware of the spiritual dimension of life. It shows me the Origin beyond the manifest practical meanings of my everyday existence. It keeps me in touch with the whole and Holy. Gentleness creates openness for the spiritual side of people, things, and events. In gentleness, the framework of practical and vital interpretations is not denied or destroyed; it only gains its rightful place in the eternal scheme of things.

Gentleness, inspired by contemplation, is more a way of respectful listening to things than of merely manipulating them. What comes to the fore in this attitude is my deepest self or spirit. Gentleness does not occur on the periphery of my life but at its core, where God is present to me. It is not an ornament, a frivolous extra for nicety's sake, but an essential part of human life as called forth by the Divine Gentleness.

If I lose gentleness, I lose a basic condition for uncovering the presence to God I already am in the depths of my being. To live in divine likeness is to live gently. Gentleness is thus a pathway to the life of prayer.

Lord, let me find back
The lost treasure of time:
Time for gentle listening to a friend,
For sharing the play of a child,
For consoling a suffering fellow man,
For thinking without strain,
For labor without pressure.
Time to delight in birds and flowers,
Blooming trees and lustrous green.
Time to enjoy music, friends, and meals,
Time to be silent and alone,
Time to be quietly at home,
Time to be present to Your mystery.
Free me from the tyranny
Of time urgency.
Let time not possess me
Neither the pressure of daily concerns.
Let me not cram every moment
With useful or exciting things
To do or say.
Let my life be a gentle preparation
For the pure and precious moments
Of listening to you
So that I may not drown
In the rushing waters
Of practical pursuits.

V

GENTLENESS, AT HOMENESS, AND
THE MEDITATIVE LIFE

A few years ago I met a young man interested in spiritual growth. John struck me from the first moment as rather tense. The way he dealt with his problems and feelings was far from gentle. He had a style of ordering his life that in no way resembled the divine style of doing things, for we read about God, *Disposuit omnia suaviter.* He orders all things graciously.

John surely did not try to order things graciously in his inner life. He was exceedingly preoccupied with his past, his future, his faults and foibles. He was always trying to figure out how and why he felt a certain way. He was almost fanatic in his effort to trace things to experiences in his childhood or to the attitudes of parents, brothers, sisters, and teachers towards him.

At times I would express my uneasiness about his constant delving into himself and his past. He would then ask, "How can I become a better person if I do not know what is wrong with me and how that wrongness came about?" It was difficult to deny what he said. I got to the bottom of the problem when he once added to his defense, "After all isn't that what the saints did? Examination of conscience was what they called it."

I knew immediately that what he was doing was not exactly the way of the saints. The saints did not look into themselves in the tense way John did. What was the difference? They were gentle because they did not see themselves in isolation. The tense introspective person sees himself cut off from nature, fellow man, and God. He experiences his interiority as isolated.

Introspection became popular in the West when the spiritual outlook of man began to wane. The waning of spirituality meant that man lost his home in the universe. Man as spirit is openness to the whole and Holy. He feels himself a small participant in the divine mystery that enfolds cosmos and history. God himself is his homeland, his most original ground. Hence man as spirit cannot look into himself as if he were isolated from everything else. He must learn to see everything in himself and in his life history from the perspective of the Divine.

In times of spiritual flowering, this attitude may communicate itself to the population as a whole. The majority of people may not enjoy the depth of spiritual experiences represented by the masters. The influence of the masters, however, is so highly respected and widely spread that it can communicate to the population at large an outlook that makes everyone familiar with this divine perspective.

People are aware of their inner happenings, but they don't take on an exaggerated importance, as may happen when the Divine is no longer present in the everyday awareness of the average person. These are the times of introspection. When God is absent, the individual in isolation may become all important. The inner peculiarities of man become overwhelmingly present. The person becomes obsessed with himself. Introspection emerges as a highly regarded technique, used by people to make contact with their lost selves. And why have they lost themselves? Is it not because they have lost contact with their divine ground? With this loss, they also lose contact with other people and things because it is the Divine Presence alone that welds all life together.

When I deal with myself in an introspective fashion, I gradually grow less gentle. For example, I may discover a certain weakness in applying myself to my daily task. As a result, my house looks sloppy, the work in my office piles up, people do not respect me, and my chances for promotion are slim. I feel a certain shame about my way of handling things. I want to improve and so I begin to look into myself to find out what in my life led to such sloppy and ineffective attitudes.

Because I live in an era of introspectionism, it is easy to find books that can guide me in my self-questioning. Enlightened by these readings or by a counselor, I may discover all kinds of incidents in my childhood that have led up to my present sloppiness. I may go back farther and farther, even to the first years of my life. I may then try to improve myself. So far so good. But something is missing. In this excellent procedure, I miss an ultimate home in which all these incidents and their consequences make sense. I may feel depressed because of what happened to me. It seems meaningless. Why should I have had such a childhood? Why should such harmful incidents have happened to me? Why should I have to cope with them?

The ultimate why I seek is the why of a final meaning. It is a why that becomes a where. Where am I at home with all these peculiar attitudes of mine? Asking this question is the same as asking where am I accepted as I am, whether or not I succeed in unearthing all these unconscious deforming influences? Where do I find a gentle and caring love that carries me as I am and makes my life meaningful in the deepest sense?

When I am merely introspective, I am a man without a home. Even the most clever psychiatric or psychological explanation cannot give me that ultimate home experience, so necessary if I want to live a life that is deeply joyful and wholly at peace in spite of sin, deviation, and limitation. When I do not have that sense of at homeness, I feel alien in this universe. The world becomes a hostile place where gentleness is absent.

When I experience no gentleness, when my faith in an infinite gentility dies, I cannot for long stay gentle myself. Feeling alone and threatened by the potential hostility of all that is not me, I necessarily develop attitudes of suspicion and defensiveness, of competition and envy. I become aggressive with myself. Lost in a universe that is no longer my home, I feel solely dependent on my own forces. I feel as if I have to whip myself into shape, to force myself to effectiveness, to drive on relentlessly. How different my life would be were I to find the mystery of Divine Presence as my lasting home.

I become gentle when I can feel with St. Paul that in Him I live and move and have my being. All things look different to me then. Introspective reflection gives way to meditative reflection. I learn that I should first of all make myself at home in the omnipresence of the Divine.

In meditative reflection I never concentrate on an isolated me. I look at myself always as showing up in the light and the love of God. Similarly I do not see people, events, and things in themselves but as they emerge and disappear within this same light and love. I dwell meditatively on myself as deeply loved and cared for by God within the situation He allows to be. When I look on my rooted, sustained, and divinely loved self, I do not experience the strain of self-preoccupation the look of introspection necessarily evokes. Rather my look becomes a gentle look, clothed with the gentleness of God Himself. I no longer feel lost in an indifferent universe. Nor do I feel the load of guilt and shame that does not find a divine redemption.

Meditative reflection thus directs me primarily toward the mysterious presence of God in all that is and especially in that dimension of the universe that is my personal ordinary life. In meditative reflection I see myself as taken up in a divine plan that manifests itself at every moment of my life. I experience a total at homeness. In and through my every day situation, I feel myself immersed in the eternal Divine Presence.

When I look at my childhood in meditative reflection, I do not see it as the ultimate explanation of my life problems. In deep faith and reverence, I hear Divine Providence speaking to me in and through the childhood God allowed to happen to me. I gently ask Him how I—so formed or deformed by my childhood history—can make the best of it. I accept my childhood—even if it entails a life long burden of neurosis and imperfection—as coming from God's hand. I am deeply aware of a divine mystery that saves and carries me in and through that childhood and in spite of it. Meditative dwelling, unlike introspection, prevents me from seeing my childhood in isolation from God's caring presence. The mystery of Divine Providence is ultimate, not my childhood history in and by itself.

Connected with the introspective stand is a certain willfulness. A harshness creeps in when I will my perfection or improvement without dialogue with my daily surroundings and past history, experienced as rooted in the mystery of God's will. As a result I tend to plan my life in isolation. I may force my projects through without taking into account sufficiently the daily divine, human, and natural situations that are my true home.

Meditative reflection means gentle dwelling on the deeper divine meanings of daily life. I center prayerfully on all happenings as expressions of the Divine Will. I try to take into account with wisdom and reverence the ongoing revelation of my surroundings. Mine is a gentle self-orientation to the mystery of daily reality.

At the best moments of my life, my willing becomes a participation in the indwelling will of God. Meditative reflection teaches me to spiritualize and divinize the common life I am living. The Divine Presence incarnated Himself in the ordinary situation of a life lived for the greater part as a worker in Nazareth. I participate in this wonder of the Incarnation when I dwell meditatively on the deeper divine meanings of my daily life. I become less tempted to ambitious fantasies about myself and my future. My spirituality becomes more trustworthy as it emerges out of the ordinary life, lived as a manifestation of the Father's will. Whatever takes me unnecessarily out of my daily life in Christ is always suspect. Such action isolates me. It tends to make me closed, proud, and the victim of wild spurts of self-centered imagination.

By contrast, on the way of meditative reflection, I begin to experience God as the Beyond in the midst of daily life. Meditative reflection implies a mindfulness that is most beneficial when balanced by a kind of forgetfulness, meaning that I must reimmerse myself repeatedly in the natural flow of daily life. Without this healing forgetfulness, I might become alienated from the transcendent dimension of God's will as manifested in the sacrament of everydayness. I should experience this reimmersion in daily life as a true homecoming, as a being about the things of my Father.

You order all things graciously.
You are the mystery
Unfolding cosmos and humanity.
You are my homeland,
My most original ground.
Your Presence
Welds all things together.
You are the caring love
That carries me
Like mother earth
Does forest, flower, tree.
Outside you
The world is a wilderness,
The universe indifferent,
The earth a barren planet
And I a speck of dust.
Your Presence alone
Is lasting home;
You are the Beyond
In the midst of daily life,
The sacrament of everydayness:
Immersion in daily duty
As flowing from your hand
Is homecoming to you.

VI

SPIRITUAL LIFE AND GENTLE REFLECTION

Reflection is
a precious gift; it enables me to look thoughtfully at
God, myself, at any experience, idea, or event that
attracts my attention.

Reflection can be analytical. I isolate the "reflected upon" from the larger backdrop of reality in
and against which things reveal themselves. I not only
cut the "reflected upon" off from the larger whole to
which it pertains; I also cut it up in its inner
wholeness, that is, I am not present to what I reflect
upon, be it person or thing, in its inner simplicity and
unity. Analytical reflection, both inwardly and outwardly, is divisive. It purposely loses sight of the
totality and goes at its object aggressively. This
aggressiveness of thought is not without influence on
my attitudes: I become more strict and precise,
warding off what does not pertain to the dissection of
my isolated object.

Reflection is not always analytical. I may reflect
on myself, others and nature to become one with a
Divine Source, mysteriously united in an Eternal

Origin. I reflect meditatively to see creation as pointing silently to the Uncreated Love out of which all emerge, each one in its own wholeness and simplicity.

This reflection is not divisive but unitive. It makes me whole; it attunes me to a mysterious totality that already is. This is a healing reflection. Far from being dissective and aggressive, it is meditative and gentle—a gentle preservation of all things as given and as tenderly held in the splendor of a Divine Presence.

Gentle reflection is a source of spiritual living. What else is spiritual life than a life of presence to a Presence that holds all things radiantly together in the Eternal Word become man? Why then is this art and discipline often neglected?

Our culture sets great store by utility, efficiency, success. It fosters aggressive reflection which helps build science, technique, and efficient organization. But one cannot rest in this predilection for the analytical. It is only one side of the story of reflection. Some analytical consideration may be useful for certain aspects of the spiritual life, especially in regard to its incarnation in my work and personal relations. Nevertheless a main source of spiritual living in its deeper dimensions is the healing power of gentle reflection.

In gentle reflection I do not center on myself as an isolated person facing the task of overcoming isolated problems and projects. Neither do I tighten my heart to scrutinize my own feelings or take stock of my petty progress. In both cases I lose the fruit of meditation. I become disquieted instead of deepening myself in an atmosphere of equanimity. I may end up with a self-centered emotional piety instead of ending up in Him, the Eternal Truth of my life.

Gentle reflection may include myself, not as isolated but as seen and centered in the light of Divine Presence. In His light I see my sinfulness and nothingness, my inability to build by human power the edifice of a spiritual life.

St. Hildegard described this condition for gentle reflection. "I ignore myself totally in body and soul. I count myself for nothing. I turn to the living God and leave all these things to Him so that He who has neither beginning nor end may condescend in all things to keep me from evil."

A gentle avoidance of any return to myself as outside the Divine Light is thus an essential condition for meditative reflection.

Gentle reflection proceeds in an atmosphere of leisure and repose. Its quiet presence to divine things is animated by a desire to be at home with God in love—a love that itself is a grace of God.

Aggressive reflection aims to master, to dominate; gentle reflection to listen, to be at one with, to be a disciple. Both kinds of reflection have a place in the life of the spirit, but gentle reflection should prevail. Meditative reflection may be compared to the thinking of Mary; analytical reflection to the thinking of Martha. As St. Augustine says in *De Verbis Domini:* "In the beginning was the Word, this is He to whom Mary listens; and the Word was made Flesh, this is He whom Martha served." And, as the Lord declared, "Mary has chosen the better part, which shall not be taken away from her" (Luke 10:4).

By now it should be clear why the way of gentle reflection can be distinguished from the aggressive way; it is the way of stillness and repose. Its aim is to go beyond the topics meditated on to a union of the deepest self with the Divine Presence. There is an awakening of the faith, a lived affirmation, a deepening and refreshing of the gift of faith already mine by Baptism. This awakened faith is a source of spiritual energy and transfiguring light; it will radiate in all dimensions of my life.

Gentle reflection awakens me from illusion. In my fallen condition, I take mirages for truth. I am ego-centered when I should be God-centered. I have lost inner wholeness, a loss that obscures the splendor of the Divine Presence in my life and in my world. This loss leaves me a victim of a multitude of illusions that distort my perception of people, events, and things. Enchanted by projects, ambitions, possessions, I become blind to God, who is my Creator, I live in illusion.

Gentle reflection implies a certain detachment from daily involvement. This distance helps me to discern the illusionary ways in which I relate to God, self, and others. I begin to awaken from illusions. I experience the Divine Presence as the true center of my life. I awaken to the true nature of reality, both created and uncreated, seeing things from within God as it were.

I no longer view men and other creatures as self-contained entities external to God, to one another, to myself. Within the Spirit of God, all created things exist in intimate togetherness with one another.

Gentle reflection is thus a means on the way to man's original state of wholeness and to a fullness of sanctity and participation in the Divine Nature.

One of the most beautiful themes of gentle reflection is that of the resplendent Divine Indwelling in the depths of my true self. At certain moments God may halt the movement of meditative reflection and make me feel the mysterious flame of the Divine Presence ever glowing within. God draws me irresistibly into the divine mysteries He himself reveals in the silent depths of the core of my being. What I learned from faithful gentle reflection becomes now one simple lived experience: any good I do, think, feel or possess does not originate in the isolated me; it is dependent on the grace of God; it originates in Him.

During gentle reflection such pauses of wordless presence may grow in frequency, intensity, duration. This experience may be so overwhelming that it grows difficult at times to engage in any reflection. Meditative reflection should be set aside at the moments God grants me the grace of a deeper mode of presence—a presence that goes beyond any limited word, image, or reflection and keeps me silent before the mystery of the Eternal Word.

Loving Trinity,
In the mystery of your love
You granted us
The precious power of reflection
On the way to at oneness with you.
Make us reflect on our lives,
On people, events and things,
Meditatively, gently, healingly.
Grant us a reflective vision
That rescues the simplicity
Which things radiate
In the splendor of your presence.
Do not allow us to center
On ourselves alone,
As if we were not held constantly
In your loving light.
Let no anxious self-reflection
Tighten our hearts,
Nor pained concern
About our petty progress.
Save us, Loving Trinity,
From the pitfalls
Of self-centered piety.
Make us attentive
To your call
Beyond reflection,
Beyond images, forms and thoughts
Into the stillness
Of a wordless presence.

VII

GENTLENESS AND DIRECTION OF THE SPIRIT

At the end of His life, the Lord promised us His Holy Spirit as a light that would illumine our lives. That light is with us always. It lights up our hearts. It lights up the situations in which we find ourselves. At some moments this divine light may shine forth in a special person, who may become our spiritual director. If he is wise, this person knows that he cannot direct us on the basis of his limited insight, experience, and study alone. All of these factors may play a role, but he sees as his main function helping us to discern the light of the Spirit in our own lives. The Holy Spirit may use some of the director's wisdom and experience to open us up to what God wants to tell us.

The truly spiritual director allows the Spirit to use his talents freely. He tries to quiet down the arrogance and impetuousness of his own opinions, pet theories, and cleverness so that nothing unnecessarily interferes with the whispering of the Spirit. If he allows the noise of his own feelings to take over, he knows he will fail to hear the messages of the Spirit that transcend the wisdom of man.

A good spiritual director thus strives to be a gentle person. Gentle with that inner calm that helps a man to distance himself from his own know-it-all tendencies so that there is room for the Holy Spirit to tell him what none of his study and experience can.

In the life of the person who comes to him for help, there may be certain incidents that repel him due to his own temperament, education, or family background. The averse feelings aroused in him may then blind him to the uniqueness of the person he is directing whereas the Holy Spirit wants him to speak to this person in a way that does not destroy but uplifts his limited God-given self. Gentleness in the director prevents such repulsive feelings from growing unchecked and helps him see behind the surface of the person to the real self beloved by God.

Gentleness is thus a prevalent necessity in a spiritual director or in anyone who at a certain moment of life is called to spiritually guide the life of a fellow man. To be sure study, preparation, experience, and wisdom are also important. But without the virtue of gentleness, such expertise may become more of a hindrance than a help. It may be used to foster only the personal opinions and prejudices of the spiritual guide instead of being made available to the light of the Holy Spirit that outshines the wisdom of man.

Gentleness is no less necessary in the person to be guided if he wants to benefit from spiritual direction.

The person should first of all be guided by the Spirit of the Lord. His Spirit speaks mainly in the Church, which is the continuation of the life of Jesus on earth, and has the fullness of the Holy Spirit. Any Christian who does not listen to the church is likely to be at odds with the Holy Spirit.

Secondly, in light of the spiritual direction given him by the Church, he must listen to what the Holy Spirit seems to say to him in his own life situation. For most people these two ways of listening give them all the direction they will ever receive. Some people, however, at certain times of their lives, may also meet a person used by God to enlighten them in a special way about the path they should follow. In all three cases, namely listening to the Church, to the life situation, and to the incidental persons who may sometimes cross our path, we need to be gentle.

Since the Fall, each of us is tempted to give the immediate needs and desires of mankind first place in our attention and efforts. This means that each of us is inclined to make ego fulfillment the ultimate guide of thought and action. This tendency is so deeply rooted in our fallen nature that it has become like second nature to us. We are usually not aware of our ego-centeredness and hence are overcome before we know it. The Holy Spirit, in and through the Church, the life situation, and the incidental guides we may meet, tries to illumine us about the prison of self-centeredness in which we are living. He tries to help us grow beyond our original blindness. He wants to show us that at least partially the way of life intended for us is still clothed in darkness.

To see that way, we may have to give up the weak but familiar light in which we are living. We are like people secluded in a room without windows working away by the light of a tiny electric bulb. Outside the room is a splendid world illumined by bright and beautiful sunshine. But we are so preoccupied with the small familiar things we are doing in the artificial light of the lamp that we refuse to go out into the full brightness of the day to discover the beauty that awaits us outside our narrow room. We become so over-involved with our limited aims that we cannot leave our light. We try to bring every new thing into the small circle of our lamp. There we analyze and evaluate it in the light of our own moods, feelings, and motivations. They are not lit up for us in the natural light of the day and inevitably their appearance is distorted.

It is for this reason that we must seek the guidance of the Spirit. He is the light of the Lord that illumines our lives. He does not speak in our isolated interiority; rather He speaks in our inner room as illumined by His presence in the Church, in the life situation, and in the incidental guides He may send to us. To receive that light our inwardness should no longer be a walled off isolated chamber. It should be like a room that receives outside light through a bright picture window. The light enters this room especially well when its windows are clean, free of dust and dirt.

We know that in daily life windows can get dirty when smoke or stale air fills the room. It is the same with our soul. The pollution of our arrogance, of our elated ego ideals, of our prejudices and inflexible positions closes the windows of our soul to the light of the Most High. Every thing the Holy Spirit tries to tell us through the Church, the life situation, or an incidental guide is taken into that dark room of our closed off interiority. There we interpret it in the artificial man-made light of our own ego-centric projects.

How do we prevent the smoke of self-centeredness from clouding the windows of our soul? The answer leads us again to gentleness and the need to develop a gentle life style. The results of the original fall of man are so deep that we will never overcome totally the inclination to put ourselves before God. Self-assertive movements will always be with us. The only thing we can do with God's grace is to temper them. The fire of the Fall cannot be extinguished but we may prevent the smoke from spreading so much that it covers our windows entirely.

We can only temper the flame of ego-excitement when we live increasingly a gentle life. Gentleness is the readiness to quiet down noise that threatens to cut us off from the voice of the Spirit. It relates not to one or the other vice or virtue, passion or compulsion, but to our life as a whole. It tries to keep our life on an even keel. Gentleness is not to be equated with the spiritual life in all its fullness. It is rather a preparation for and a fruit of this life.

Likewise gentleness does not assure the effectiveness and depth of spiritual direction; it is, however, a necessary condition for this effectiveness.

Gentleness both in the spiritual director and in the person directed by him is thus a necessary condition for true openness to the Spirit. If we have at some moment in our life a personal spiritual director, this is to be seen only as an incidental event. We should be gentle about the lack of personal direction too. If we begin to desire or search inordinately for a personal spiritual guide, we fail already in the gentleness the Holy Spirit asks from us. We decide in advance the way in which *we* think our lives should be guided by Him. We feel it necessary that He should manifest Himself in a special person and not simply in and through the general direction given by the Church and the life situation. We are no longer gently open to the possibility that He deems it better for us, as for the great majority of people, not to have a personal director over and above His speaking to us in the general direction given by the Church, its structures and institutions, and through the life situation.

We must live in deep faith that the Divine Master is present to us in the Church, in our life situation, in our soul. He is present there as a Spiritual Director with infinite gentleness. He is always ready to guide us in the light of the Holy Spirit as long as we are willing to listen. This willingness expresses and embodies itself in a gentle life style. Living in gentleness is making room for the voice of the Divine in our lives.

Praise you, Lord,
For your splendid promise
To send the Spirit
Light of Light,
The gracious One
Whose radiation
Pierces like a lazer beam
The wall we build
Around our hearts.
Lovely Spirit of the Lord
Dim the turmoil
Of frenzied words.
Clean away the arrogance
That pollutes the atmosphere
Of gentleness and love.
Temper our self assertion,
Soften our unbending stand,
Save us from deceptive dealings,
From policies of lust and pride.
Enlighten us, confused and caught
In argument and angry thought.

VIII

POVERTY AND GENTLENESS OF SPIRIT

Poverty and gentleness of spirit both relate to the spiritual life in its fundamental meaning. This meaning is found among other places in Mark 12:28-34. There Jesus says, "This is the first commandment: Listen, Israel, the Lord our God is Lord alone! Therefore, you shall love the Lord your God with all your heart, with all your soul, with all your mind, and with all your strength." A scribe then turns to Jesus and adds, "Excellent, Teacher! You are right in saying, 'He is the One, there is no other than he.'" Jesus praised the scribe for his understanding.

To be wholly present to Him as Lord alone, with all our heart, with all our soul, with all our mind, and with all our strength, to no other than He, we must be poor in spirit.

Poverty of spirit is more than material poverty. We may be without many possessions yet possessed by cravings for countless things. That craving makes us restless. A restless heart is mirrored in a restless spirit, in a mind flooded by vain images that ceaselessly emerge from uncurbed desires. The spirit of poverty frees our minds from the turmoil of idle musings by lessening our attachment to things as ultimate.

Material poverty is more familiar to us than poverty of spirit. Being reared in a materialistic society, we are inclined to understand all things—even religious poverty—in a merely materialistic way. Of course, poverty of spirit has its outer material aspect. We will see later how this more visible poverty—if freely lived for God—is meant to facilitate poverty of spirit.

Poverty of spirit makes us present to God alone. It carries us beyond the idols we have set up in life and breaks their hold on our feelings, thoughts, and fantasies. No longer are we divided by these false gods. The spirit of poverty heals us; makes us whole, at one for the One. The more steadfastly we walk in the light of poverty, the more we gain in awareness that there is no other than He.

Jesus describes the oneness that results in our presence to God once we become poor in spirit. "Therefore you shall love the Lord your God with all your heart, with all your soul, with all your mind, and with all your strength." The love for God that flows forth from this oneness of presence is like water flowing from a spring.

Love means the going out of our lonely being to what is other. Love for God is a homecoming. It is return to the source, a regaining of the lost core of our lives. All human life is a seeking for that mysterious other, that lost home, that forgotten source, that hidden core.

This other is sought after in love and friendship, or even mistakenly in success and status, in entertainment and travel, in drugs and parties, in precious and rare possessions. Strange and manifold are the ways human love travels in search of fulfillment. Strange because normal love would seek its fulfillment only in a meeting with persons.

Once someone or something seems to offer the promise of fulfillment, love bends our whole soul, heart, and mind in the direction of that thing or person. We do not see anything else. To others we may seem "mad." They do not understand what love does to its victims.

This desperate search for fulfillment on the human level gives us some inkling of what will happen to us the day we hear the call of the One, the day we come to see, because of our inner poverty, that—as the scribe said—there is no other than He. The scribe was praised by Jesus for saying this. For indeed there is ultimately no other than God alone who keeps all people and things in existence. The love we are by nature, the love that drove us in so many directions, necessarily turns us now to the Lord alone as ultimate. He alone ultimately draws our seeking nature, for He is Other, Home, Source, and Core.

To be at one for the One, to know and taste with our whole being—like the scribe praised by Jesus—that there is no other than He, is the aim of poverty of spirit. The tender flower of this total presence blooms in a climate that is mild and even, a climate of equanimity. A spirit absorbed in the Divine is a gentle spirit. Therefore the person who wants to travel the long road that may end in this absorption must begin to strive after gentleness of mind and heart.

Gentleness and poverty of spirit sustain each other. Without poverty of spirit no inner gentleness is possible and without gentleness of spirit the gift of presence to the Lord alone eludes us.

Little wonder then that poverty of spirit is a cornerstone in the spiritualities of all great religious. Jesus calls the poor of spirit blessed. Religious of all traditions make some vow or promise of poverty. The great masters, too, speak ceaselessly about this poverty of spirit. Their images are striking. They talk about emptying or voiding the mind of all thought not related to the Source. Empty mind, no mind, naked mind, inner nudity, void—these are only some of the words that turn up again and again in their writings. The mind should be empty of thoughts in so far as they attach us to anything as ultimate besides God.

Poverty of spirit is the aim of all asceticism, for, as the spiritual masters know, only such poverty readies the soul for the gentle receptivity in which the Divine Beyond may reveal itself. The asceticism of poverty is fundamentally an asceticism of inwardness. The test of its effectiveness is the climate of gentleness it leaves in the soul. Gentle single-mindedness before God is the fruit of poverty of spirit. He may then deepen that purity of heart, that single-mindedness, by drawing the soul into His own ineffable at oneness.

Outer practices of poverty take second place to inner poverty. The whole worth of such practices hinges on what they do for growth in poverty of spirit. Do they facilitate or hinder the voiding of our minds? This is the one question worth asking in relation to religious poverty. Over-aggressive involvement in social issues, immoderate party going and socializing, obsession with rules and regulations, compulsive hoarding of possessions, fanatic excitement with passing fads, addiction to mass media—all throw the mind in frenzy. None allows our spirit to stay poor and gentle.

It is for this reason that all great spiritual traditions advise a certain moderation in life style, a kind of secondary outer poverty that facilitates growth in poverty and gentleness of spirit. Poverty of life style—freely accepted for God—fosters a gentle life style, relatively freed from rigidity, fanaticism, and over excitement. For poverty of life style implies mortification of certain expressions of uncurbed passions, feelings, and desires and of the thoughts and fantasies that flow from them in the restless mind.

We are not only spiritual men striving for intimacy with the One. We are psychological and social beings who strive after other interests that may or may not be connected with our striving after Divine Union. The striving for intimacy with the One can be served by freely choosing and maintaining a certain poverty of life style. The danger is that we may take such freely chosen styles of poverty as the ultimate meaning of religious or inward poverty. In that case the deepest original meaning of poverty of spirit may be lost.

Let us think for a moment about some forms of poverty that can be mistaken for poverty of spirit. The kinds of poverty that come to mind are five: *proletarian, spartan, social, apostolic, communal.* None of these forms of poverty, either taken singly or together, is identifiable with the essence of spiritual poverty.

One striking form of poverty that emerged in the West with its widespread advance in industrialization was proletarian poverty. Its essence implies the absence of cultural and physical surroundings and means that facilitate human and spiritual growth, and, therefore, it can never be elevated to an ideal. The blight of proletarian poverty is one of the terrible consequences that laborers had to suffer due to the striving for power and possession of Western mankind. Its scorch was one of the factors that estranged man from presence to God. It would thus be nonsensical and dangerous to foster or imitate proletarian poverty in order to gain a poor and gentle spirit in the sense of Jesus and the spiritual masters.

Another kind of poverty is spartan. History tells us that the Spartans were formed by tribes of warriors. They practiced a frugal life style to harden men for battle. Today, still, certain ambitious people may live a life of rigid frugality and self-denial to prepare themselves for competition in the arena of economy, politics, or academic performance. While there may be a certain goodness in this frugality, it is not primarily oriented toward the development of gentle receptivity, or a poor spirit that expects all things from God alone. On the contrary this frugality may lead to an extreme self-centeredness, to the development of a harsh and violent ego that uses spartan poverty to dominate its surroundings.

A third form of poverty manifests a higher inspiration. Certain people may desire to share in the poverty of a population in order to show how such sharing, if done by all, could reduce the poverty of a country or a minority group. The aim of such social poverty is again not first and foremost to come to a poor and gentle spirit that unites one intimately with the One. Rather social poverty aims to create a more perfect humanity that holds as ideal a social equality that can redeem mankind from all its sufferings.

Certain followers of Christ may choose to engage in apostolic poverty. For example, in order to win a certain population for Christ, they try in accordance with some of His teachings to make their home with that population. If the people are poor, they generously share their poverty; in this way they hope to be accepted by them. This acceptance may lead in turn to the acceptance of the Christian Church and religion. While such apostolic poverty is praiseworthy and while it may even be facilitated by an already existing religious poverty, it is again by no means the essence of poverty of spirit.

A last form of poverty is communal. In this case people decide to share all the goods they have in order to create a commune or community where people will get along more easily because the striving for possession no longer as readily divides them. Again this kind of poverty, however beautiful an ideal, cannot be called the essence of poverty of spirit. This essence relates primarily to inner poverty and gentleness of spirit which ready man to be at one with the One and to freely accept and practice a certain moderation of life style that facilitates and safeguards this inward poverty and gentility.

SPIRITUALITY AND THE GENTLE LIFE

You are the One, the only One,
And yet I crave for countless things
With restless heart and mind,
Deluged by fierce desires
That know no bound.
Carry me beyond my idols;
Walk with me
In the softening light
Of simplicity of heart,
Of single-mindedness
From which flows forth my presence
Like fresh water from a spring.
Eternal Other, forgotten Source, mysterious Core,
Tend in me the tender flower
Of holy presence
That gently blooms
In the mild and even climate
Of equanimity.
Grant me a poor gentle spirit,
Not lightly thrown into a frenzy
Of passing fads, obsessive hoarding,
Addiction to mass media
Or sins of Spartan poverty
And social fanaticism.

IX

GENTLENESS AND INVOLVEMENT

Spiritual life, while inclining me to solitude, leaves ample room for involvement in society. Involvement may harm the gentleness of heart so beneficial for presence to the Divine. Loss of gentility now and then is to be expected. Interruptions of the gentle life style are unavoidable. Involvement in work and play, in social movements and human encounters, may lead to emotional upsets. Such occasional outbursts do no lasting harm to the gentle climate that fosters spiritual growth. More serious is constant tension. When turmoil and tension wrack me for too long a time, it becomes difficult to remain open to the Holy. Certain involvements can seriously diminish the gentleness I need for a life of communion with God.

Clearly I cannot stop involving myself in society. Perhaps the reason for my tension is that I am involved in a task that is not right for me. One reason for choosing the wrong task may be that certain charitable works are lauded as "the" ideal expression of all Christian life and that I am a soft touch for such exclusive claims.

For example, some women can contribute best to society by remaining at home to create a good social environment for husband and children. Doing that for the Lord, they grow spiritually. It may be that a certain kind of woman, giving herself wholly at home, cannot do much more outside the family. She may need her extra time for prayer, rest, and recreation, if she wants to keep serving her husband and children effectively in a relaxed and gentle way.

One day some of her friends in the parish may begin to recruit people for various charitable works. They ask her to assume a leading position. In their excitement they seem to suggest that this kind of social involvement is "the" involvement for any gifted dedicated parishioner. But this woman is already involved socially all day long. She is involved in her family. Many women could take on other duties, but she cannot. Her strength and inner resources are limited. Special problems in her family, unknown to outsiders, exact already a heavy toll.

If she were to take on more, she would fail God's will as expressed in her limitations. Taking on what goes beyond her power could lead to excessive tension, irritation, and even false guilt feelings about her lack of effectiveness in charitable activities. She would soon lose inner gentleness. Without gentility she would easily betray the Divine source in the core of her being, the hidden well of what little wisdom and strength she can display at home. It would then become difficult for her to handle wisely the social issues raised within her family.

What is true for this mother in her family and spiritual life, can be true in a different way for a secretary, a teacher, a parish priest, a nursing sister, a writer or artist. All of them are faced with the question, "What kind of social involvement can I take on within my limits?" Not everyone is called to be an administrator of charities, a fighter for civic justice, a politician, war protester, missionary, parish official, or social organizer.

Spiritual life, to repeat, may incline a person to some kind of social involvement, but it does not imply the same kind of social life for everyone. The involvement that is clearly the will of God for you may be as clearly a failing of God's will for me. This kind of failure, when lasting, may make me lose gentleness of heart. To do something that goes against my total make-up demands an excessive forcefulness, a tight control and repression of my spontaneous being. It is precisely this aggressive self-exertion that destroys gentleness of heart.

Even if I have found the right kind of social involvement, I may still lose gentleness because of the way in which I involve myself. I may do the right thing with too much ambition, anxiously, with agitation and fear that I may not look as conservative or progressive as the next guy. Thus I need to question my motivation. What really moves me when I am involved socially?

When I feel an attraction to some kind of social involvement, I must examine what this means for my spiritual life and the gentle climate it demands. I must also question my vital life of impulsive likes and dislikes. What I impulsively or compulsively want to accomplish is influenced by my past as well as my present environment. Do I want to become involved because my family or friends have instilled in me false guilt feelings for not being engaged in a social enterprise they value so highly? Do I feel inferior to them? Do I need to prove myself in a task that goes beyond my capacity? Is this work really what I can do best? These are only a few of the questions I may ask myself before I take on a specific work.

The answers to such questions can never come from the work itself and its general justifications. A social or missionary endeavor may be splendid in itself. A large number of people in the church may rightly involve themselves in it. Philosophers, theologians, and representatives of the social sciences may justify it. Mass media and religious orators may blast away at those who do not participate. But the one question for my spiritual life is whether this splendid work, done or justified by all those others, should be done by me.

To find the right answer to this question I must reflect on how I live my spiritual life within the limited sphere of possibilities God granted me. I must consider the self-deceptions that may throw me into activities that can diminish inner gentleness. Blind compliance with the social enthusiasm of orators and mass media can lead to the sin of self-abuse, that is, the physical, psychological and spiritual abuse of my real self, in which God expresses His will for me.

Just when I think I am motivated spiritually to engage myself in some widely acclaimed undertaking, I may be a victim of some unclarified likes and dislikes in myself or swayed by popular opinions of others. Spiritual motivations are always imbued with right or wrong feelings, and desires that may be unconscious. I must not believe in advance that even my spititual motivation is the right one. Has my life of desire been purified by my reason, enlightened by faith? I must ask myself if my spiritual desire to serve is influenced by the acclaim of a progressive or conservative crowd or by the true claims of my inner self. Such questions are not primarily theological but personal. They are questions of a lived spirituality.

To become involved in social issues in some specific way is a question of my personal experience of my own life of faith and of my own mental and practical power to handle such works. How do these two experiences, my experience of my own spiritual life at this moment of my development, and my experience of my involvement, influence one another? Is this influence good or harmful for my life of faith as unfolding in the limited self I am?

Others have put such questions to themselves—the saints and spiritual writers like Teresa of Avila who tried to live a life of faith while being involved in the reformation of her order. I can turn to their writings to learn the art of reflection on my life in the light of the mystery of my unique calling.

Spiritual reflection from the viewpoint of the life of faith implies distancing myself from the work as such and even from the general justification or popularity of this work. I put my awareness of the general desirability of a missionary or social enterprise momentarily into brackets so as not to disturb the personal question. My own unique life of faith can then question itself and answer itself whenever a work is offered to me as a chance for involvement. The person to pose the question is not the enthusiastic defender or the zealous propagator of the work, but I myself who has to give an answer to myself before God, assisted perhaps, in some cases by a spiritual director.

This does not mean that all general considerations about the desirability of social missionary works are rendered invalid. Such considerations have their place. They offer necessary information and possible motives for the many tasks Christianity should be open to. They cannot tell me, however, whether I, as this specific, unique Christian, should engage myself in the work under question. The wide acclaim attached to a social or missionary work can serve as an alibi that covers up the real issue of what this involvement will mean for my unique life as a whole. I may use this alibi to escape spiritual self-questioning when a work is lauded with great enthusiasm. Such plaudits fire me up.

The trouble is that emotional excitement about some holy undertaking may be at odds with who I really am and with what I can do. I begin to live in a tension between two opposing feelings that can tear me to pieces; on the one hand, my real feelings emerging from the hidden attraction of my unique spiritual calling, which I ignore; and, on the other hand, self-alienating feelings, engendered by the social or missionary enthusiasm of others. Such tension makes inner gentleness impossible and in the long run may ruin whatever involvement I take upon myself whenever I fail to consider, in light of God's plan for me, what my best possibilities and real motivations are.

To see God's will for me, the light of human reason is not enough. I must ask the Holy Spirit to illumine me.

SPIRITUALITY AND THE GENTLE LIFE

Spirit of my Lord,
You want me to dwell in society
With a gentleness of heart
That keeps me open for your light.
Prevent me from being caught
In any social movement,
In any missionary enterprise,
No matter how beautiful and holy,
That would not be a movement
Meant for me from eternity.

Give me the wisdom and strength
To be wholly present to my daily task
Instead of being more present to undertakings
God did not will for me.
Grant me the humility
To accept the resources
God has allowed me.
Soften excessive forcefulness,
Tightness and anxious self-exertion.
Infuse me with a wisdom
That clarifies my motives,
That liberates me from the curse
Of enslavement to popular opinion.

Let the splendor of the works of others
Blind me not to the hidden splendor
Of my own endeavors.
Let me not abuse my self
Merely to please others
By taking on good works
They are engaged in.
Forgive me and heal me
When I abuse the general acclaim
For a great and holy enterprise
As an alibi to escape
My own calling.
Holy Spirit, teach me
To be your gentle follower
In all situations.

PART TWO

GENTLENESS AND AGGRESSION

X

GENTLENESS AND AGGRESSION

Gentleness is a main condition for spiritual living. Can I then allow feelings of aggression in my life? What about attack, taking the offensive, feeling angry? Can I be indignant as Jesus was when he ejected the vendors from the temple? Can I be gentle of heart like my Lord and still combat those who make light of divine truth? Dare I speak out as He did against scribes and pharisees?

Aggressive feelings can be wholesome and human. They may keep us alive and dynamic in situations that demand a sharp, swift approach. The Holy Spirit does not paralyze what emerges spontaneously in human nature. My aggressive potency is not cut off short but set on a new course. The Spirit turns this potency in a new direction.

I may wrongly consider all aggressive feelings to be less than human. They all may seem incompatible with the spiritual life. Wanting to live in gentle presence to the Holy, I may begin to repress my awareness of any anger and aggression that emerges in me.

SPIRITUALITY AND THE GENTLE LIFE

It is true that nearly all believers who want to live gently before God have difficulty coming to terms with their aggressive feelings. I too tend not to take these feelings in stride. Instead of working them through, I turn them off. Not daring to see them for the human feelings they are, I may malign all indignant feelings as unworthy of a spiritual person. The price I pay for such denial is incalculable.

Repressing awareness of my feelings may not be an act of bad will on my part. Therefore, in spite of such self distortion, the life of grace can keep growing deep within me. However, this power of grace may not be able to shed its light in this distorted area of my emotional life. Grace wants to break through to the aggressive potency in man, not to destroy it but to purify it from selfishness and turn it into a healthy readiness to do battle for the Kingdom when necessary.

Not only may I deny aggressiveness that is misdirected; I may even deny my ability to be aggressive. Because aggressiveness is removed from my awareness as quickly as it comes up, I cannot place it under the transforming light of the Spirit who dwells in my heart.

Anxious repression does not do away with aggressiveness. I can hide but never destroy this potential of my nature and its inevitable upsurge in my life. I may mask aggressiveness with gentleness, but it still comes out as muffled violence. Others sense that my gentleness is a fraud to take advantage of them, as does the smooth salesman of poor merchandise.

This masking of aggression may not be a conscious forgery on my part. My intention may be honest, my desire to be gentle genuine. What is pretended is a lack of anger that is really there. I alone am the victim of such unconscious pretense.

Perhaps I fell into this trap because I pushed myself too fast and furiously into the role of the gentle saint. I skipped the work of catching my angry feelings, of bringing them honestly to light, of bearing with them patiently, of giving the Holy Spirit room to mitigate them and turn them toward the Kingdom.

Gentleness does not deny anger and aggression. On the contrary, it helps me to bear with even that unreasonable aggression I cannot as yet overcome. Gentleness draws from this affliction a humility that in turn deepens the gentle life style. Being gentle with myself helps me to bring to the fore in the right way, at the right time and place, my reasonable indignation without hurting others unnecessarily. It drives aggressive feelings to the surface, never pushes them underground.

A gentle life style is difficult to maintain when unresolved anger lurks within me. Anger, driven underground, poisons my spiritual life. Aggressive feeling when repressed cannot spend its force wisely and moderately. All it does is turn inward and thrive as a hidden explosive power—a counter style of the gentle life ready to pervert true gentility. When it bursts out finally, it does so in an uncontrollable destructive way.

Anger should be allowed to come into the open from the beginning and spend itself in a wise and moderate way, for instance, in a forthright talk with a good friend or spiritual director. This openness gets rid of beginning anger and allows the gentle life style to be taken up again. After anger has been aired and dispersed in an acceptable way, gentleness may deepen.

The gentle life style should be the usual climate of my life. Moments of anger, expressed in the right way to the right person, should only be interruptions of my basic style of gentle spiritual living, passing incidents that do not touch the calm inmost region of gentleness that prevails. This inmost source of gentleness in the core of my being is my presence to God in faith.

Aggressiveness should not become a lasting style of life but only an incidental emergence—necessary in certain social situations for defense of the rights and truths of the Kingdom, for the unique role I am there called to play. Necessary also for psychic relief and for keeping the gentle life style pure, that is, unmarred by hidden aggressive feelings.

The wages of repressed anger include not only a distorted spiritual life but also, in the long run, poor psychological and bodily health, damage to my togetherness with others, and diminishment of my apostolic effectiveness. As I try more and more to live for God, I see that I should not be concerned about health and effectiveness for their own sake but for the sake of His Kingdom. The Lord may take away my physical and psychological health. He may choose for me a life of suffering, letting me share in the lowliness of the kenotic Christ, who emptied Himself of glory.

To many of us this grace may come when we grow old. No one can choose this mission of suffering for himself. What I can and should do is accept the normal suffering I meet every day in my task and surroundings. I may add to this some mortifications and disciplines of my own, but for the rest I should follow the common way of fostering my psychological and physical health in such a way that I can be available to God as a channel for His generosity among men.

God wants me to use the means Providence allowed to keep relaxed, radiant, and healthy in mind and body. If I cast off this common way, instead of using it gratefully, I may be less able to serve as a channel and instrument of His loving will for man.

One way to maintain and foster healthy readiness for the Divine is to accept and work through my feelings of anger and aggression. Insight into these feelings can free me for a more gentle life and make available hidden energy, talents, and abilities for the Kingdom.

Taking a healthier spiritual view of my potentiality for anger and aggression seems in general to foster better health of mind and body. Owning instead of disowning my angry upsurges, my temperamental moods, my sometimes aggressive disposition seems to lead to more effectiveness in the work God asks me to do. Life is fuller spiritually. Religious cultural participation improves. I move through my days with more health and vigor until that moment when God may call me mainly to a life of suffering in and with the kenotic Christ.

Thus to deal spiritually with aggression requires grace and wisdom. We shall reflect concretely in the chapters to follow on how to detect, expose, spiritualize, and wisely express aggressiveness without hurting others. This chapter touches only the beginning of the problem of how to spiritualize anger and aggression. So far we only commented on the general compatibility of a gentle life style with intermittent moments of anger and indignation.

You ejected vendors
From your Father's house;
You assailed scribes and pharisees.
We adore your holy indignation
Nourished by love,
Love for the Holy One,
Love for the Kingdom,
Love for mortals
Burdened unbearably.
Gentleness was behind your indignation,
Infinite was your readiness to turn anger
Into love.
Praise to you, Lord Jesus,
For assuming all of human nature,
Also anger and indignation;
For setting them on a new course,
The course of the Kingdom.
Let us not malign our feelings
But lift them into the light of the Spirit.
Instead of driving anger underground
Teach us to take its sting away.
May our lives no longer be poisoned
By anger we refuse to resolve.
Keep us relaxed and radiant in mind and body,
Wide open channels for your generosity among men;
Our health and gentleness no longer marred
By hidden feelings of hostility.

XI

GENTLENESS AND SPIRITUALIZATION
OF ANGER

All people
get angry, saints and sinners alike. Saints too are
human. Holiness does not take away humanness. Our
Lord Himself shows by His indignation how human
He was. Feeling annoyed, angry, aggressive is therefore as human as feeling sad, delighted, loving, tired,
or lonely.

Everybody gets angry. This may not always be
apparent, but it is so. The only exceptions are not
saints or gentle people but men and women whose
brain functioning is impaired. Gentle persons get
angry like everyone else. The difference is that anger
and aggressiveness do not dominate their lives. They
may be incidentally angry, usually at the right time
and in the right way. Also they seem to know better
how to handle their aggressiveness.

Growth in the spirit does not whittle away my
capacity to feel angry or aggressive. Neither does it
lessen my need to respond in some way to that
feeling. Growth in the spiritual life does not help me

to accept my aggressiveness as a human feeling that is undeniably there. The unfolding spirit of man, moreover, offers each person a wider divine view of life. It is from this perspective that I may see in a new light the persons, events, or things that arouse my anger and aggression. From this wider view my anger either subsides, lessens, or finds its right expression in the angry situation. This divine view itself is born not in anger but in gentleness.

Anger and aggression are likely to emerge in response to discomfort, tension, pain or frustration. We see shades of this in the angrily crying infant who feels wet, hungry or bothered by a safety pin that has become unclasped. He expresses his discomfort wildly without measure. He is his anger, as it were. He cannot as yet develop a wise and gentle view of life, nor can he place his discomfort meaningfully in the context of the total situation and thereby mitigate anger, if not disperse it completely. An adult, who has grown in the life of the spirit, can do that—at least in principle, if not in fact.

It is not enough to enjoy this wider spiritual vision of life; I must also know my anger and its source so that it can be illumined and tempered by this spiritual vision.

A first condition for this spiritualization of anger or aggression is knowing fully that I feel this way. Next I need to find out why I am feeling so. Only then can I do something about the way I feel in the light of my gentle vision of life. My angry "feeling against" can be tempered by a deeper "feeling for."

My feeling threatened by certain situations can be lessened by my experience of being saved, cherished, and cared for by an Eternal Love.

Still it is difficult to realize and accept peacefully that I feel angry and aggressive. A false idea of what spiritual life should be like has perhaps made me feel ashamed, guilty, or anxious about my aggressiveness—so much so that I don't dare to admit to myself how angry I sometimes get.

I may have pictured holiness as an angelic state of life, never touched by violent upsurges of emotion. Even when I own up to the anger that arises in me on certain occasions, it may still be difficult to pinpoint its original source. It takes insight, prayerful reflection, and patience to find the links between recurring occasions of moodiness and the annoyance, anger, and aggression they evoke.

Another condition for dealing wisely with aggressiveness is to show gentle respect for the pace of progress that grace, nature, and the given situation allow in my life. Everyone's pace is unique. In some people spiritualization goes fast; in others its pace is painfully slow. Most people show an irregular pattern. Their spiritual growth is marked by ups and downs, peaks and valleys. Others again show a regular, rhythmical progression.

Within certain limits our pace of progress can be improved. However, our individual nature, unique situation, and personal gifts of grace set definite limits to the possibility of improvement. When I try too impatiently to push beyond these divine limits, my attempts backfire. Things get worse instead of better.

A premature attempt to spiritualize anger and aggression has the opposite effect: these feelings are denied, overlooked, repressed. They then grow wildly, unchecked in the depths of my personality. They may also come out indirectly in sly, mean, repulsive ways, disguised as pastoral zeal, holy concern for the salvation of souls, fanatic dedication to my own mission or social apostolate, where I try to force everyone to participate, whether or not the person in his uniqueness is called to this task.

To deal wisely with anger, hostility, aggression I must accept the limits of progress that the Infinite Love allows in my life. In this regard, it is good to remember that the life of grace is not the same as the fullness of spiritual life. The inner life of grace is the fountainhead of the spiritualization of my life as a whole. Spiritual life is the gradual permeation of my whole self—in its spirit, ego, and body dimensions—by the grace that God pours out in the core of my being. This flowing out of His gracious presence into all of my experience and action is a gift too. However, my personality make-up may offer obstacles to this divine flow and prevent or slow down my total transformation. Excessive anger, repressed aggression, and hidden hostility are all hindrances. They prevent me from becoming an attractive sign and radiant incarnation of divine gentleness and love.

God wants me to try to overcome these obstacles. He wants my attempts to be in accord with the pace of transfiguration He has allowed in my life. For reasons of temperament and for environmental causes beyond my control, I may be unable to remove these obstacles. My pace of progress may be so slow or irregular in the area of overcoming anger and aggression that I may never master these problems during my lifetime.

While in this world I may not be granted the fullness of an exemplary and attractive spiritual life; this in no way means that I will be less graced in the depths of my being. God's grace will fill my soul in the measure that He grants me the gift of loving Him with His own love. No matter how poorly I succeed in mastering my spontaneous upsurges of anger and aggression, grace keeps growing in me. For God what counts is only my good will and the joyful humility with which I accept my daily failure.

Loving acceptance is not resignation. It is the peaceful readiness for spiritual transformation to take place in God's good time here or in the hereafter. It is submission to and cooperation with God's dynamic transformation of my life whenever and wherever His grace enables me to be transformed.

Refusal to grow beyond unmitigated anger, when doing so is possible without excessive tension, is a refusal of grace itself. Such a declination would be a sign of bad faith that would hamper not only the full expression of grace in my life but also the original flow of grace in the inmost center of my being.

Thank you, Lord,
For consecrating our feelings
By showing anger,
By being sad, delighted, lonely.
Teach us how to rule aggression
Instead of being ruled by it.
May anger surge at the right time,
Come out in the right way,
As your anger did.
Grant us an eternal vision
In which passing insults lose their sting.
Anger they may arouse, but no longer
Rage and fury that insanely want to hurt.
Let angry feelings of rejection be tempered
By an awareness of being saved and cherished
By an Eternal Love.
Grant me the grace of respect for the slow pace of progress
An Infinite Wisdom allowed in my life.
Don't let me push beyond borders
Fixed for me from eternity.
Let no hidden hostility
Disguise itself as zeal
For your Kingdom.
Inspire all people of noble purpose
To search for means that may diminish
The hostility that consumes humanity
Gentle Grace, transfigure a world of warriors
Into a land of love.

XII

GENTILITY AND EMOTIONAL RESPONSE

All of us are born with the ability to feel angry or gentle. Usually such instantaneous responses are not freely chosen. We picked these reactions up from others long before we could talk, or for that matter understand what was being said angrily or gently by the people around us. While we could not yet comprehend, we could sense the angry and gentle moods, feelings and deeds of father and mother, brothers and sisters. Without them having to tell us, we learned from them on the spot how to act angrily or gently.

As children, we listened to the way in which they responded to our own feelings, especially those of aggression or gentleness, when we dared to let them come out. Maybe we were lucky enough to be born into a family that allowed us to bring our feelings out into the open without playing any of them down. They took in stride both our tenderness and aggressiveness. This did not mean that they gave into whatever we were angry about; it is just that they did not punish or condemn us simply for the fact that we felt that way. At other times, when we showed gentleness or expressed a need for gentleness on their part, they would not make us feel childish, weak or unmanly. Then, too, they let us freely know how they felt. At home they created a climate in which it was easy for us to know how they felt and what we ourselves were feeling. They realistically accepted the fact that all kinds of feelings may spontaneously emerge in human beings outside the immediate control of their will.

Each one in such a family could show how he felt without being condemned and threatened for that. We would help each other to grow in the art of expressing feelings in ways that led less and less to misunderstanding and hurt of each other.

The result of this climate of relaxed self-expression is an overall gentleness, only sporadically pierced by expressions of anger and aggression. Because the latter feelings are expressed at their first emergence, they do not have time to build up inwardly into a sudden outburst or explosion. The telling of a dissatisfaction becomes more and more like a giving of information about what is beginning to build up inside. The other can take that information into account; it is then easier to rescue or restore the style of gentleness.

In such an atmosphere, we would learn early in life that it is all right to feel gentle and loving and all right also at times to feel angry and aggressive. Such a family wants honestly to know how the children are feeling. They want their children to know that they love and accept them no matter how they feel. They do not want to stifle their feelings or to pretend feelings they do not have simply to please them.

Parents may have been secured in this attitude of letting-be by a parish or congregation where the gentle life style and its conditions were preached and lived as an essential part of the Christian art of redeemed spiritual living. Their school too and the school their children attended may have been permeated by this Christian respect for all human feelings—a spiritual tolerance that prevents the repression of anger and makes the gentle life possible.

Like most people, however, I may not have been that lucky. Perhaps my family, and the people in my school, church, and neighborhood, were afraid to admit the emergence of angry feelings in themselves or to tolerate the angry feelings that arose in others towards them. They may not have experienced the redemption of Christ in regard to their life of feelings. In this area the freedom of the spiritual person may have eluded them. As a result my life of feeling may have become unchristian and crippled. Not experiencing redemption in this area, I may have grown so fearful that my feelings might not be acceptable to any other person that I do not dare to allow them to come through even in the presence of people who are really for me. I may have a hard time feeling and expressing either gentleness or anger to my true friends with the same freedom with which Christ and His disciples expressed such feelings.

I should not blame my family, parish priests, teachers, schools or community for my emotional impotence. They did not know any better. They meant well. They may not have received a wise initiation into a fundamental spirituality that would have helped them to bring their whole life, its emotional dimension included, under the redemption of Christ, who lived in their hearts and whom they may have loved dearly. They too were victims of their own fear of feelings and of the fear of those who brought them up. They cannot be blamed for having been born and reared in a culture in which a transforming, all pervading spirituality was often replaced by sophisticated abstractions and pious commonplaces.

As I assess my situation, I should humbly adore the God of history who allowed culture, Christian and otherwise, to unfold along uneven and sometimes deviant paths. I should accept that God temporarily allowed this impoverishment of the spiritual life to happen in my life and that of others. I should even tell Him that I humbly accept the suffering of emotional impotence, if that is to be my cultural cross to the end of my life, in spite of my attempts to grow beyond it. Such surrender makes me dear in His eyes. He will fill me with grace even if this grace will not yet effect a spiritual transformation of my personality as a whole here on earth. In that case the fullness of a spiritualized life will be granted to me in the hereafter.

Such acceptance not only prevents bitterness, self-depreciation, and crippling guilt feelings; it is also the best beginning of a spiritual growth that may eventually liberate me from my inability to respond freely and openly to people I rightly love and trust.

Acceptance of my limits helps me to feel compassion for those who brought me up and who may suffer more than I do from the same emotional impoverishment they fostered in me, unaware as they were of the riches of a responsive spiritual life. I should thank my Lord again and again for the revealing insight He now grants me as an undeserved gift. I should ask Him for the grace not only to change myself but to help create a healthier, more gracious and spiritual atmosphere in which gentleness becomes a possibility and also where true anger is allowed to be felt, expressed and wisely dealt with in the light of the spirit.

As a beginning, I must stop feeling one way and acting the opposite way when the situation does not make this truly necessary from the viewpoint of compassion or wise diplomacy. When I feel angry I must not smile sweetly or freeze sullenly. I must learn instead to be humble and courageous enough before God to let my feelings come out—straight, honestly and simply, yet wisely and not destructively, if the situation allows me this freedom of expression. Surprisingly when I learn to communicate my feelings at their first emergence to those whom I can trust, it will become easier for me to express them in a modest and relaxed manner, which may restore the atmosphere of gentleness.

It is precisely when I deny my anger or pretend the opposite that it might grow inwardly out of proportion; it can no longer be enlightened and mellowed by the life of the spirit. My trusted friends, not having received the slightest clue that I am growing mad, may unwittingly add fuel to the fire. My denial and their misunderstanding may finally lead to aggressive outbursts and unreasonable displays of rage, no longer in proportion to the incident that suddenly, like a spark, touches off my accumulated madness. Such displays may poison the atmosphere for a long time. They make reasonable interaction difficult; they may even make any later manifestations of gentleness suspect as pretenses that hide anger and aggression.

When I feel angry or aggressive with a good friend, well meaning family member, or trusted acquaintance, I should let him know in some way, so that he is aware of my mood or feeling and can take it wisely into account. This openness will also help him to feel trusting when I am gentle with him at most other times of our togetherness. Neither when I feel angry should I get cold and sullen and withdraw my attention and affection from the friend or comrade who makes me angry. I should be like Yahweh was with His chosen people. He let His people know how angry He felt when they sought after false gods or flaunted His commandments. At the same time He made them feel that he did not withdraw His gentle love and lasting attention from them. The covenant remained.

Jesus dealt in the same way with His disciples, Judas included, and even with His own mother. He never made them doubt His lasting gentle care for them, yet communicated straightforwardly His sadness, disappointment, indignation, anger or dissatisfaction. He showed how He felt when they misunderstood Him, quarreled with one another, kept children away from Him, or tempted Him to go against the Will of the Father.

Briefly, if I am really angry like Yahweh or Jesus, I have to let it come out straight and wisely when possible and beneficial for all concerned. If the situation makes it impossible or unwise to do so, at least I can talk it out with a friend or some understanding acquaintance. If such persons are not available, or even if they are available, I can still speak it out or write it out for myself, run angrily around the block, pound a punching bag, or take an aggressive swim to get it all out of my system. I must, in short, never allow anger and aggression to bottle up in my soul and so to paralyze my potential for trustworthy gentleness to myself and others.

Once anger and aggression are out of my system or out in the open, I can cope with them. I can lift who or what angers me into the light of my spiritual vision. In that light my anger may melt, especially when it proves to be a mere self-centered, ego competitive anger or an anger based on the easily threatened insecurity of a self that has not yet found through spiritual growth his security in God alone.

In the light of the spirit my anger may also show up as a righteous indignation about a temporal injustice done to me or others. The same light of the spirit may show me, however, that my indignation became too absolutized and overwhelming because I looked at this incidental injustice in isolation from the mystery of Divine Providence who allowed this painful moment to be in my life or in human history.

Grant me, Lord, the wisdom of acceptance
Acceptance of anger I am unable to contain;
Acceptance of a life crippled and fearful
Because parents and teachers misunderstood the wisdom
*   You taught;*
Acceptance of any misunderstanding instilled in me
By well meaning others.
They tried to follow your teachings
As well as they could.
But you allowed their eyes to be dimmed.
Let me remember them in compassion.
If you call me to be with children
Make me as open about my feelings
As you were with your disciples,
As Yahweh was with his chosen people.
Lord, create around me a climate of gentleness
In which each person can express himself without fear.
Let me not be tempted
To force others to pretend to feelings they do not have
Simply to please me, to make me feel good.
Teach me the art of redeemed, spiritual living.
Grant me trustworthy friends to whom I can reveal
Aggression and anger before they become too much to bear.
Teach me the right means to mitigate my anger
So that my soul may be free again for your presence.

XIII

RELIEF OF ANGER AND
GROWTH IN GENTLENESS

True spiritual life may lead to gentleness with self and others. This slowly acquired gentleness emerges not from a fear to displease people, not from a need to be liked, not from a desire to foster a career, to look good or to get rid of feelings of anger, irritation, aggressiveness. Gentleness starts from the acceptance of where I stand as a poor man before God, with my smoldering anger, my aggressiveness, my resentment.

Fake spiritual life does not admit to these feelings; it does not accept them and try to live with them while quietly mellowing a little day by day. Fake spiritual life starts from an idealized picture of myself. "From now on I have to be the perfectly holy person approved of by everyone." Unconsciously I may add to this ideal image: "If I never get angry, others will never get angry with me."

This secret expectation changes the orientation of my life. No longer is my main concern God's love; it shifts to a concern for being liked by people. Mine is no longer a God-centered but an ego-centered life. I begin to build my personality on the image of the "nice holy fellow," liked and revered by all. Since this is the image I live by, any show of anger, even the slightest irritation, seems to tarnish my "holy" status. Being revered by all is a way to be safe. Any irritation I may evoke in others is felt as a threat to myself. I *must* avoid anything that brings disesteem upon me. I feel forced to play the "unruffled gentle guy" role to the hilt.

The price I pay for this role-playing is immense. I can never be myself. Constant attempts to fool myself and others cost me enormous energy. Not growing in true spiritual life because of a false start, I drift into a superficial show of sweetness. I lose out with those who might have been able to like the original limited me but who do not like me now because they are unable to find out who I really am.

If I am fortunate enough not to fall into this trap of role-playing, I may be less anxious about showing the anger I feel. This feeling does not license me to purge the anger from my system at any time or in any way that strikes my fancy. Lack of restraint hinders the unfolding of spiritual life as much as the self-deception that I never feel angry. Naturally, it would be deceptive to engage in displays of kindness with people who make me furious. But neither does it further my spiritual growth to let off steam indiscriminately.

It will be difficult to exercise restraint without damage to myself as long as I close myself off from my spiritual openness to the whole and Holy. This openness gives every incident its limited place in my life. If instead I live only in the here and now, every insult or injustice looms up as overwhelmingly important.

There is little difference, then, between either bottling up my angry emotions or letting them out of the bag by kicking the furniture, smashing a teapot, or lashing out at any unfortunate creature who crosses my path. This outburst may relieve my pent-up anger, but it does not promote my growth in gentleness. On the contrary, I begin to develop a violent style of life.

My emphasis is on the instant relief of anger here and now. I overlook the fact that the repeated acting out of aggression in numerous here and now moments will have a long-term effect on my life. Rewarded by the pleasant feeling of relief I get whenever I let people have it, I may feel the urge to be even more aggressive the next time the pressure of anger builds up inside. Every time I act out my aggression without restraint, my inner, resistance against violent outbursts is lowered.

Immoderate venting of anger may also mean that I have to work it up and express it before experiencing relief. Remnants of this worked up anger and its expression remain in memory and fantasy. Such remnants make me more sensitive to minor stimuli to anger. After many such experiences, I become easily provoked and I may explode more readily. Before I realize it, I have become an angry explosive person, often indulging in resentful fantasies and perceptions that keep me on edge. I'm always on the lookout for the wrong word, the wrong move. At the slightest provocation, my anger flares up. Such vigilance makes gentle relaxed presence to the Sacred impossible.

The spiritual person neither bottles up his anger nor releases it through unrestrained aggressive words and actions. In the beginning of the spiritual life, the healing power of the Holy Spirit and the eternal vision He imparts may not be mighty enough to dissipate in time accumulating anger. Therefore anger may be dammed up, resulting in chronic muscular tensions. In such a case, it may sometimes be advisable to let go, to let the anger out by kicking an old chair, running around the block, or allowing myself to burst out in the presence of a good friend. I should realize, however, that this is only an emergency measure—an exceptional emotional release I should not become addicted to. Otherwise its repetition may turn me away from the gentle life style.

Angry self-expression gives temporary relief even if the person I am furious with does not get hurt or does not know about my aggressive words or actions. To vent my fury makes me feel better, but it does not really drain the deeper layers of pent-up anger. In the long run repeated unrestricted expression of anger lowers my resistance to already present aggressive tendencies.

Those who share my anger may reward me with approval when I display how I feel in explosive words and gestures. They find vicarious relief in my expression. The approval I read in their face or hear in their words may spur me on to more intense outbursts. The next time I am with people who feel the same as I do about persons and situations, I may find stronger words to express my anger. More and more I become a person prone to anger who has at his disposal a growing inventory of aggressive responses.

Another experience of relief may contribute to the build up of an aggressive personality. If the person I wanted to get to has been hurt by myself or anybody else, I may feel a new pleasant release of tension. For a while my desire to attack him may lessen. When I get angry the next time, I impulsively seek for the new kind of relief I felt before, now by trying to hurt others directly or indirectly. Should this happen again and again, my aggressive habits may become so strengthened that I find it almost impossible not to try to hurt people I feel angry with.

If I want to grow in gentleness, it might even be wise to watch myself when I see violence in the movies or on television or when I hear a person speak aggressively. Anger and aggression are contagious. Watching or hearing violence makes me much more apt to allow myself to be that way too, especially when violence is perpetrated for a holy cause. The latter gives me a lofty pretense to nourish my anger, to vent it wildly, and still feel holy. This attitude may partly explain the violence indulged in by crusaders and pious persecutors of witches, heretics, and public sinners.

As we said before, we should not bottle up angry feelings by playing the role of the "holy person" who never feels angry. Now, by warning against an aggressive acting out of such feelings, do we not contradict ourselves? Not really, if we remember the distinction between verbal aggression and talking about my feelings.

If I attack someone with words and actions, I provide myself, him, and bystanders with strong stimuli for more aggression: I create an angry and aggressive atmosphere. It is a different case when I merely describe how I feel, saying, for example, "I feel really angry now." Telling the other I am angry is informative. It may clear the air between us. My honest telling may make him aware that he inadvertently hurt my feelings more than he intended. He is less likely to hurt me again. I may feel even better when my information prompts him to explain that he had not really meant to hurt me.

In other cases such exchange of information may not help at all. Perhaps the other person really wanted to hurt me or he may be so thick-skinned that he called me a "cry baby" for telling him. In that case it sometimes helps to talk the incident over with a good friend, a spiritual director, or a counselor. The ultimate solution, however, is to gradually learn to lessen my anger by seeing how relative its annoying source is in the light of my presence to God. As soon as I feel upset and angry with people, I should try not to indulge in aggressive fantasies about what I would like to say or do to them; rather I should begin to work on these feelings in the light of spiritual wisdom and revelation.

SPIRITUALITY AND THE GENTLE LIFE

Lord, save me from the need
To be loved by all, to win acclaim
For a gentleness I don't possess.
Save me from a piety
That can't admit hostility
Smoldering in my soul.
Let me mellow day by day
Following your gentle way.
When things unsettle me
Remind me they are allowed to be
By an Eternal Spring
From whom all things flow forth,
To whom they all return
After their allotted time.
Whittle away pious pretenses
To release my anger furiously
On deviants and evildoers,
Forgetting I too am but a sinner
In your sight.

XIV

GENTLENESS, ANGER AND
AFFECTIVE ISOLATION

The best way of dealing with angry feelings is to raise them up to the light of the spiritual vision God grants me. This movement implies making the objects of my anger and aggression relative, that is, putting them into a perspective that is divine and eternal.

As human spirit illumined by the Holy Spirit, I should neither deny my anger nor act it out indiscriminately. To deny my anger would be an act of pride, a haughty refusal to acknowledge before God my inner disharmony and poverty. To save my pride and make my pretense of saintliness come true, I would have to role play the perfectly harmonious holy guy. I may be so successful at this game that I actually come to believe the role I play. I begin honestly to think it is the real me and not a pretense. I am no longer aware of anger and aggression. Both are totally outside my control. Since I am no longer aware of their existence, I will be unable to mellow and spiritualize them by placing them against the horizon of the Eternal.

Letting aggression burst out wildly is no solution either. On the contrary, as we have seen, such action leads only to my getting angry faster. In the end, I may turn lastingly into an angry, aggressive person. Such would be the sorry outcome of such repeated outbursts.

The way of spiritualization is a long one, like a slow winding path. It is the way of gradual transformation of my whole person in the light of grace. I may easily confuse this way with its final result—total spiritual renewal in Christ. Therefore, it is wise to realize that the fullness of this transformation is unlikely to ever be ours during this lifetime.

Confusion between the finite way of transformation and its final end is harmful. We may try to be at the end all at once. The danger of this try is that it inclines us to pseudo-spirituality and pseudo-gentility: namely, we try to bypass the slow winding road upwards and go straight to the top, grabbing at once the splendor of the vision from high on the mountain of total spiritual transformation. This willful attempt can end only in illusion.

We are like travelers in the desert, deceived by a mirage of the oasis we are thirsting for. We act as if the mirage of the oasis is reality, as if the cool water is already ours to enjoy. Consequently, when we strive too anxiously after a spiritual life, we fall easily into the trap of denying our real anger and aggressiveness. We substitute this easy denial for the slow and painful way of the spirit—for humbly becoming aware of our anger and aggression, for patiently putting such feelings in the perspective of the spiritual vision the Holy Spirit gives to us if we are open to Him.

If we pretend to be gentle while we are not, we affect a pseudo-gentility that slows down our spiritual travel. Pseudo-gentility is based on a lie we may be unconscious of. A lie, as we know, can be maintained only by means of other lies that cover up the first one. This is true not only when we tell a lie to others; it is even more true for the lies that are at the basis of our private life, especially when we fail to see that we are lying to ourselves inwardly.

There are many devious ways by which we may try to keep the lie of gentleness alive, ways that twist and deform our inner life. The presence of such deformation in a number of pious people helps us to understand why such words as "spirituality," "piety," "devotion," "holiness," "righteousness" carry a bad connotation for many wholesome men and women. They may have had to face too many twisted fellow men who were the victims of their own quasi-spirituality and sweetness. Anyone who sensed the basic lie in their life felt repelled by the spirituality they preached. Yet these victims themselves may not have been guilty of the perversion of their life. They could be casualities of a well meant but misleading religious education or formation.

One bad means to maintain the lie of pseudo-gentleness is that of affective isolation. I try to avoid getting involved in any way with persons around me.

I feel that as long as I do not really care about them, it may be easier to keep my cool. I can for a much longer time maintain my gentle guy status. Avoidance of any real involvement with friends or acquaintances may be seen as a first step towards the deformation of my inner life. Keeping things exclusively on the surface in every relation with others is bound to deprive me of healthy open interaction, even with people I can trust and like. In this total withholding of myself, I am ultimately the loser, for wise moderate involvement with others may help me to see some of my mistakes and limitations, as well as some of my good qualities, more realistically. I would see more of my real self in the mirror of others' honest reactions.

Practicing the trick of affective isolation in order to keep perfect self-control may also make it impossible for me to see the unique revelation of Christ in others. Neither in this case can I be a vehicle of Christ, who wants to reach persons through my caring presence to them.

The fullness of a secure presence to people is possible only against a spiritual horizon. When I am really with people, all kinds of emotions may be evoked at times, also feelings of anger and aggression. Feeling in and by itself is blind; it knows no border; it tends to take over, to engulf my whole person. I am tempted at such moments to identify my whole being with a strong momentary emotion. Momentarily at least my feelings absorb me instead of I absorbing them wisely and harmoniously. Emotion can then become self-destructive. In this light it is understandable why I may come to fear my aggressive and angry feelings and the open exchange with people that might give rise to them. The question is how can I not deny these feelings, how can I allow them to be evoked in normal human interaction, and still cope with them in such a way that I will not be overcome by them?

I can begin slowly to cope with these feelings by developing a spiritual horizon. To understand how such an horizon helps me to mitigate anger, let's take another look at the flare-up of anger.

Imagine someone insults me injustly. The anger I feel is so vehement it overwhelms my awareness of everything else. I can think of nothing but my anger. My mood of anger towers above any other calming insight, human concern, gentle consideration, or wise reminiscence that I may have had at my disposal before this moment of rage. Anger has taken the central stage and eclipses anything in my mind that could moderate this madness.

How can I prevent this violent flare-up from happening again and again? One way is by nourishing in my inner life opposite thoughts, feelings, images and motivations that become so much a part of my awareness that they present a counterbalance when anger overwhelms me. Such counter thoughts must be so alive that they cannot be easily pushed off stage by feelings of anger. Moreover, these inner convictions must be of such a scope that they present my awareness spontaneously with a different and wider horizon against which the event that evokes my anger shrivels in size and importance and assumes naturally a limited and different meaning.

No convictions are of a wider scope and power than spiritual convictions. They offer an eternal perspective, an infinite horizon. The person who, with God's grace, really tries to live in this horizon is no longer so easily overwhelmed by any feeling related to fleeting earthly incidents.

When this grace becomes mine, I may be able to see the event that evoked my anger in the perspective of a spiritual horizon. Surely it was an insult. But is this passing insult in this passing world really of such importance that I should get so worked up about it? Is it not a blessed occasion to suffer with my Lord humiliation in love for my Father in heaven? Is it not a possibility for penance for my sins, a unique chance of purification of my self-centeredness, a lesson in detachment from this age and the vain glory it can give to man?

This spiritual horizon will only be powerful enough to calm the stormy sea of angry feelings when I have really made it my own over a long period of time. It is only by regular spiritual reading of Holy Scripture, meditative reflective prayer, dwelling on spiritual masters, and participation in the liturgy that I create, with God's grace, an alive world of meaning that may in time diminish the overwhelming power of anger and aggressiveness. The spiritual horizon, which emerges in me in the long run out of these repeated moments of spiritual dwelling, becomes a living awareness.

At the same time I must try slowly to develop another habit; it too must become second nature for me. This is the habit of relating the emotions that arise in me—in my interaction with people—to my emerging spiritual horizon, a horizon that opens me up to the Eternal, the Infinite, the Divine Presence, the redeeming love of my Lord. In this meeting, emotions sooner or later lose their power to engulf me. I am less likely to become livid with rage. In this way the spiritual man to some degree overcomes the self-destructive power of an overwhelming anger. He no longer has to avoid real interest in others. Neither does he have to deny his feelings. He gives his emotion the right place in the light of the divine vision the Holy Spirit grants him, if he keeps faithfully dwelling on the words of the Church, on Holy Scripture, on the spiritual masters.

SPIRITUALITY AND THE GENTLE LIFE

When I am the brunt of scorn and derision
Help me to lift my anger into your light.
I need a wider spiritual vision.
My sight is narrow,
My feelings twisted.
I cannot see the wider meaning
Of each event.
I hide in my shell
Like a frightened tortoise
Instead of placing my feelings
Against the horizon of the Eternal.
I pretend to be gentle
When I feel upset.
I live a lie
That twists and deforms my inner life.
However poor, it is this life you love.
Not perfect self-control,
Not phony sweetness,
Not fearful isolation
But an honest response
Of who I truly am.
Now I can hear your invitation
To lift these feelings into your light.
Now I can mellow my anxious strife
To reach perfection over night.
Help me to relate what I feel
To your redeeming love.
Let me not become livid with rage
But illumined with the gentle vision
That grants each event its rightful place.

XV

GENTLENESS, ANGER, AND SELF-MASTERY

A definite
hindrance to healthy awareness of anger and aggression is the arrogant need for immediate and total
self-control. This need arises especially when I con-
found true spirituality with the false spirituality of a
willful mastery of self and surroundings. I live in the
illusion of maintaining absolute self-possession and
unruffled gentleness in all possible situations. To
maintain this illusion means that I cannot allow
myself to do, feel, or think anything that threatens
the facade of my gentility.

True spiritual life, as we have seen repeatedly, is
based on the humble and relaxed abandonment of my
whole self, with all its faults and limits, to my Lord.
The true spiritual person expects spiritual growth
from God alone. He is the source of whatever
self-transformation may take place. In false spirituality, by contrast, man is the center. The
pseudo-spiritual person sees holiness not primarily as
one's gratuitous transformation by the Divine but as
a feat of self-mastery.

SPIRITUALITY AND THE GENTLE LIFE

This is not to say that self-mastery is totally uninvolved in the way of transformation. Self-control is not, however, the central event, the core of one's renewal. Grace is. A certain relaxed self-mastery is merely a remote preparation for the way grace works with man. Self-mastery may also be a secondary effect of the grace already working in the core of my being.

Grace is elusive; it is mysterious. Presence to this mystery of grace is foreign to present-day man. His allegiance is to a culture of conquest and mastery. His idea of the successful spiritual life is construed in terms of the same mastery that gained him the admiration of peers and parents, teachers, colleagues, supervisors, wife and children.

The man of mastery may not care that much about being liked by people. His excessive need is to be praised and admired, if not worshipped. He imagines the saintly person as a man of iron will, a paradigm of perfect self-control, never betraying anger or irritation, rightly earning universal adoration. He feels he is this man, at least potentially.

The criterion for his status of "spiritual superman" is the outspoken or whispered awe of his fellow men. He feels secure and affirmed as soon as he senses that others feel he is the guy who does not lose his cool in the most trying situations. This awe he treasures. He fears losing it by a show of anger that would expose him as being as human as the fellow next door. Such anger he fears would mark the loss in him of the control everyone marvels about.

In his mistaken mentality, he thinks a holy man may never lose control. Any show of anger or aggression is seen as evidence of a loss of self-mastery. He looks, therefore, with trepidation on any feeling of anger that emerges in him. He experiences it as dynamite, potentially explosive; it may lead to the loss of his poise and self-possession. Worse, it threatens to explode the myth of what he fondly imagines to be the marvel of his spiritual life—the will power that has kept him impeccably gentle. However, his pseudo-gentility is more like the straight-laced behavioral correctness of the proverbial butler than the meekness of the Lamb of God. It misses the graciousness and refinement that flows spontaneously from a graced interiority. He shows instead the angularity that results from rigid training and willful self-control.

Pseudo-spirituality is often accompanied by pseudo-gentility. When we strive after the life of the spirit, we may develop parallel with it and secondary to it a pseudo-spiritual and pseudo-gentle personality. Both are perversions of the true life of the spirit, of the relaxed gentleness that is the steady support of a graced inner life. We might pause here to ask, where does this pseudo-spiritual life come from?

In periods of excessive distress, political battle, or fierce competition, we may experience a regression from relaxed spiritual presence to anxious tense self-preoccupation. We are inclined to use any ploy that may enhance our self-esteem. Among other things, we may also play out the attractive appearances of self that are the fruit of our spiritual life and of the gentle behavior that goes with it.

Say we have through spiritual living acquired pleasant virtuous manners. Something happens that angers us deeply. At that moment we regress to a state of fearful self-protection. Though we no longer feel spiritual, we may cleverly display the external signs of gentle virtuous behavior to make a good impression. If we do so repeatedly, we may set in motion a whole self-developing system of pious appearances. This back-up system of piety constitutes a secondary pseudo-spiritual life. We may all suffer from it to some degree.

In some a fatal shift may take place. The pseudo-spiritual life may become primary while true spiritual life becomes secondary. This may happen in persons whose parents, teachers, or religious community have implicitly communicated that pious appearances are most important in life: one must always look good, no matter the situation.

Others again never develop either a spiritual life or true gentility. From the beginning they cultivate only the outer marks of gentleness; they play at being gentlemen in outward imitation of the gentle manners of the saints. An inner emptiness hides behind their outer gentility, no matter how accomplished their smooth behavior. Gentleness is feigned to further self-centered aims or to foster political or business enterprises within or without a religious setting.

A final and frequent form of lasting pseudo-spirituality results from the pressure of exalted spiritual ideals that in reality deny the all too human side of man. The person so afflicted wants to reach spiritual perfection too fast. Not being able to attain this aim, he plays at being saintly and perfectly gentle. Unfortunately he takes his play for reality. His false spirituality is marked, moreover, by much hidden pride, often disguised as humility.

Perverted gentility gives rise to many abberations of one's emotional life. It poisons, mars, and maims life spiritually, psychologically, bodily. True gentleness, on the contrary, cleanses, yields and mellows my whole being.

Pseudo-gentility, as we have seen, causes me to pervert anger and aggression instead of spiritualizing them. If I live a pseudo-spiritual life of proud, perfect self-mastery, I am cheated of any awareness of feeling angry. For years I have been trained inwardly by my "saintly self-picture" to put down automatically and instantly any feelings of anger or irritation that may arise in me. The purpose of this unconscious inward training process is to keep me absolutely free of any recognizable threat to my saintly self-image. After a while, living out of this image becomes second nature.

Repression of any awareness of aggressive feelings cheats me also of any possibility of growth in real virtue in this area. A virtuous act done out of love for God is a free act. I make a free choice in the face of my emerging anger and aggression. If I freely choose to accept this anger as mine, to work it through as well as I can in the light of the grace and vision God grants me, I grow a little in real spiritual life, even if I am not yet able to keep my anger and aggressiveness within reasonable and charitable bounds. If I keep giving this graced free virtuous response, I grow every time a little bit more in this art of putting my anger in a spiritual perspective.

After some time of numerous repeated acts, I may even notice a slight difference in my angry feelings and outbursts. They may seem a little less explosive and overwhelming. I experience what could be called a "just-noticeable-difference." I keep trying to live on that new level of being a little less explosive. A while later if I keep trying quietly, I may experience again a "just-noticeable-improvement" on the new level of living I have reached. Usually the change is nothing more exalted than that. But keeping on this steady course after many such just-noticeable-improvements, people who have not seen me for many years may notice that I am a somewhat changed person.

More important than this noticeable change is the steady inner growth of my spiritual life. The repeated awareness of my human weakness keeps me humble and receptive before God. It enables me to pray with a contrite heart and helps me to experience the necessity of redemption. I experience more intensely than ever the graciousness of God's love. This meditative self-presence makes me also gain in the wisdom of true self-insight and in insight into the human condition. As long as my pretentious saintly picture of self put down all angry feelings immediately, I was cheated out of using these occasions as stepping stones for growth in wisdom, grace, and virtue.

Prevent me, Lord, from confounding
The mystery of your life in me
With willful self-mastery.
May my gentleness not be a facade;
May it flow forth from my inmost center
Where you reign supreme.
Save me from becoming
A proud paradigm
Of perfect self-control,
A spiritual superman,
A sick worshipper
Of poise and self-possession.
Save me from the pressure
Of exalted ideals
That deny my humanness.
Let my soul not be maimed
By perverted gentility
Grant me the gift to pray
With a contrite heart
And to be saved daily
From the deception
Of pious fantasies.

XVI

GENTLENESS, THE DEADENING OF ANGER, AND THE EMERGENCE OF ANXIETY

Another means to maintain pseudo-gentility is to deaden the anger and aggression I feel but cannot admit. This is a most pernicious means to deal with anger, for it affects all feelings. Paralysis of anger works only when I remove myself from all of my emotions, also from the uplifting ones like love, wonder, tenderness, admiration, enthusiasm and devotion. By paralyzing my feelings in this way, I silence my aliveness. I put myself under a lasting anesthesia; I walk around as if I were drugged.

No spontaneity, sensitivity, or creativity can survive this doping of my emotional life. Worse than this, I withdraw a whole dimension of life from the influence of grace. By killing emotionality off, I make it unavailable to the vital service of the Kingdom. I make it impossible for the Lord to shine forth through me both in the genuine anger and the gentility I may feel in my everyday relations with fellow men.

How can I even relate to them humanly if I don't feel? How can I, paralyzed, drugged and frozen, feel how people are feeling? How can I let them feel in and through my alive personality how the Lord empathizes with them? My paralysis removes me as a feeling person from the presence of God in the world, in myself and in others.

It is healthier to feel angry with God, as the man Job and some of the prophets did, than to have deadened all my feelings in order to escape the emotions of anger. My pseudo-gentility covers my paralyzed life of feeling as a death mask. This mask may fool people but not for long.

If I do not admit my anger or don't try slowly to spiritualize it in the light of grace, it does not go away. Neither does it just sit there inert. It somehow must come out. The distorted way in which it will come out is no longer under the control of my spiritual life or reason. It will therefore be a crippled expression. The twisted outbursts of anger and aggressiveness in the pseudo-spiritual person may be so distorted that it will be almost impossible to see that these expressions have something to do with the real feelings of anger.

When I live a pseudo-gentle life, I twist and pervert my feelings of anger automatically without awareness. Perverted anger and aggression, hidden behind a grotesque mask of gentleness and piety, eventually poison my whole spiritual life. I begin to suffer strange guilt feelings. Not knowing where they come from, I try to fit them into my warped self-image of the kind and saintly man divinely chosen. I may ascribe my misery, subsequent headaches, and digestive troubles to fallen angels allowed by God to tempt His friends. Or perhaps I feel God himself is purifying me to elevate me to greater heights than I have already reached. Through it all I may pride myself because of the gentle smile I wear bravely in spite of my torments. I don't suspect in the least that this phony smile may be at the root of my troubles.

It is important to recognize such pains and twisted expressions as part of a process of pseudo-spirituality that always is at work in fallen human nature. By contrast, true spiritualization, as we have seen, is the effect of grace; it is marked by peace, simplicity, and a natural gracious gentility.

When anger and aggression are not spiritualized but bottled up they may be twisted by the pseudo-spiritual person into pietistic anxiety.

Pietistic anxiety is derived directly from feelings I have deadened out of so-called religious motives. I did not work these feelings through in the light of God's loving understanding and forgiveness. We call such anxiety pietistic because my pseudo-spirituality inclines me to give it a pious meaning that ties in with my exalted self-image.

The feelings I refuse to own and work through in God's light may be manifold. They may be sexual, proud, arrogant, possessive, envious, jealous—briefly, they can be any feelings whose very existence in me I feel to be incompatible with my illusion of righteousness. We are interested especially in looking at feelings of anger and aggression denied in myself because of a contrived gentility. Anger and aggression perverted for this reason are a major source of pietistic anxiety.

Anger twisted into pietistic anxiety can take two forms: crude anxiety or complicated hidden anxiety.

I can feel crude anxiety mentally and even bodily. I may feel mildly fearful or even panicky with a feeling of going to pieces. The experience of anxiety may be so strong that I feel cramps in my muscles; my heart may flutter, my neck painfully stiffen. I may also feel shaky, alternately chilly and flushing. My stomach may be upset to the point of nausea. I may have one of these bodily feelings or a blending of some or many of them. They may be slight or strong.

In the case of pietistic anxiety, the feeling of fear may be accompanied with a sense of doom. I may think I am condemned by God. I feel already the suffering of the damned. Unaware that denied anger and aggression are the source of my anxiety, I grope anxiously for any explanation that can make sense out of my suffering. If I don't buy the condemnation explanation, I may fall back on the dark-night-of-the-soul, special-divine-trial, or demonic explanation.

Sometimes a person who is deadly afraid of losing his gentleness may experience an anxiety attack when suddenly emerging anger threatens to disrupt his gentility. The belief that it is the devil who fills him with this anxiety may lead to the illusion of demonic obsession or possession. This belief in the special interest of the devil in him is compatible with his saintly self-image. After all, were not the saints themselves tried out by the devil? For him belief in demonic obsession may imply far less loss of self esteem than seeing and accepting the fact that he suffers from emotional disorder as a result of faulty living. The conviction that the devil plays his game with him is an added protection against the discovery of the real source of his anxiety: the anger and aggression he does not dare to admit, the mask of gentleness he feels unable to take off even for a moment. In extreme cases pseudo-gentle people tortured by repeated anxiety attacks may ask for an exorcism to be performed on them.

In many cases pietistic anxiety is not felt in this direct crude form but manifests itself as a complicated hidden anxiety. The impact of crude anxiety is mitigated and dissipated in a variety of emotional upsets and ailments. They may be relatively quick in their appearance and disappearance. Or they may be of long duration, persisting sometimes during one's whole life.

In some cases the pseudo-gentle personality under the pressure of inner anxiety develops rigid sets of severe unbending judgments or stilled habits, inflexible customs, and obstinate ways of acting, strangely at odds with his frozen smile, benign commonplace pious words, and forced gentility.

He may also develop other signs of emotional disturbance, such as depression, obsession, phobias, severe insomnia and so on. Again because of his tendency to pietistic explanation of all anxiety, the pseudo-gentle Christian may ascribe these disturbances to supernatural causes.

While such disorders may succeed in diminishing the feeling of anxiety, they are highly destructive. They make peace of heart and mind impossible. It becomes increasingly difficult to relate to God in a quiet, prayerful way. Such false explanations interfere with one's harmonious pleasant interaction with others. They tend to block severly one's smooth functioning in nearly all dimensions of daily life.

While such painful symptoms lessen the impact typical of crude anxiety, they tend to yield new forms of anxiety. This added anxiety calls forth again more of these symptoms. And so it keeps going on in a vicious circle unless the pseudo-gentle person is able to face his denial of the anger that led to his anxiety. In serious cases only a well prepared spiritual teacher or director or a professional person may be able to help the victim gradually discover the ultimate source of his anxiety and its many symptoms.

Pseudo-gentility is thus one of the great powers in life that can beget and nourish anxiety. Pseudo-gentility breeds perverted anger and aggression. As such it is the mother of a wide variety of emotional disorders. We may consider pietistic anxiety as the first crippled child of a make-believe religious gentleness that compels us to deny to ourselves how angry we really feel. All other disorders, some of which we may consider in more detail, are related to this anxiety.

Gentleness, the Deadening of Anger,
and the Emergence of Anxiety

> *Let me not silence my aliveness*
> *Nor withdraw my feelings from your grace;*
> *Guard me against putting on*
> *The death mask*
> *Of a feigned gentility*
> *Because I dare not own*
> *My anger and aggression.*
> *Let me not deaden all feelings*
> *Nor escape even my occasional anger with you.*
> *Let me not twist anger and aggression*
> *Into pietistic anxiety*
> *That poisons body and soul,*
> *That fills me with a sense of doom*
> *And the suffering of the dammed.*
> *Let me not accuse a fallen angel*
> *Of a self-distortion*
> *That is mine alone.*

XVII

GENTLENESS AND DISPLACEMENT OF ANGER

When I strive too anxiously after a spiritual and gentle life, I may become selective of the occasions in which I allow myself to show anger or irritation.

I may, for instance, remove my anger from any person, organization, or movement that looks religious to me: the Church, the clergy, the religious community, a charitable movement in my parish. I instead displace my anger on to a person or movement that is not so clearly linked with the religious sphere or to people who know anyway that my show of gentleness is a farce.

For example, I transfer or displace my seething anger from a pastor who frightens me to my frightened daughter whom I caught sneaking out late at night. I somehow sense unconsciously that my wife and children know from former outbursts that I am not really that gentle. I have no image to lose here. This example explains why certain people are devils inside and angels outside. Though I may have a glimmer of awareness of what I am doing, I usually am unconscious of what is going on.

A pseudo-spiritual person, who always seems gentle, can suddenly get angry at someone for no apparent reason. He may become furious because of an imagined hurt or may get unreasonably mad at a minor insult or forgetfulness.

I may have been hurt often by people or organizations I thought I had to be gentle with because of their religious meaning. These old hurts may have accumulated and exaggerated over the years. I may let loose the immense anger built up in me as a result of all this accumulated anger onto someone or something else, not in the least linked with the religious institution or people that evoked my anger in the first place.

Because I want to save my self-image of saintly gentleness, I must find something that I consider to be clearly unholy. Then I can allow myself to release all my pent-up anger without losing my feeling of righteousness.

The favored occasion of my unbridled release may be a public sinner, the "filthy" rich, the oppressors of the poor, the picture of a scantily clad girl, a daring movie, the foolishness of teen-agers, a wayward child, an alcoholic, a drug addict or a clergyman who happens to be "way-out." Of course I may rightly have reservations about the principles and behavior of these people. I may also feel a certain justified anger with them. But what gives me away is the ferocity with which I crusade against them; in this campaign I am totally unlike the meek fellow I usually seem to be.

All the anger I did not dare to admit to myself because of my pious self-image now comes down as hell and damnation on those I consider not to belong to the chosen people.

The exaggerations and accumulations of anger in the pseudo-gentle person can be quite violent when they emerge. They can become a lasting problem. This person's lifelong rage may be transferred to pagans, convicts, leftists, capitalists, misbehaving students. He feels in such cases that anger is holy and allowed. He may spend a lifetime splattering these "unholy ones" with the loosened debris of his old anger.

A person may also turn anger to himself, becoming full of selfhate and suffering as a result—serious depression. Not knowing the real source of self-hate, I may explain it as deep humility, inner mortification, pangs of holy guilt, or as a dark night of the soul, a special trial sent by God to His beloved one. Such explanations save my pious self-image.

At times I may direct this self-hate outward to sinful people; I begin to hate them instead of being aware of my self-hate. I may become convinced that the God of justice and vengeance is after them and I am His standard bearer. Or I may do something totally different. I may become unaware that I hate myself or that I hate them. Instead I imagine that they hate me. This is called projection. I project the hate I feel for myself onto them, as if it were a hate coming from them. If this projection is blended with piety, I imagine that God allows them to crucify me like they crucified Jesus, that I, the well intentioned gentle one, am chosen to suffer at their hands. A pseudo-spiritual life can thus be destructive of the entire personality and can even in severe cases drive men to madness.

As we mentioned before, many people who honestly strive after a spiritual life develop both a true and a pseudo-spiritual life, a true and a pseudo-gentility. Fortunately in most of them the true spiritual life prevails; pseudo-spirituality and make believe gentility may emerge only in moments of stress, anxiety, insecurity, and true or imagined persecution.

It is important, however, to realize that I, as many others, may have developed a pseudo-spiritual life parallel with my real spirituality. This pseudo-spirituality forms a consistent structure of thoughts, feelings, motivations, images, attitudes and habits. This hidden structure of personality lies in waiting, as it were, and can come to the fore in certain critical situations without my being aware of it. Not realizing its insidious nature, I may mistake it for the real thing.

Good spiritual initiation helps me to become aware of this make-believe spiritual life. I may become increasingly able to spot its emergence in times of crisis and insecurity and to cope with it instead of being taken in by it.

The main intent, consciously or unconsciously of my pseudo-gentle life, is to shift anger and aggressiveness to movements, people or situations that I can be angry with without losing my self-image of the holy person who remains gentle as long as God's honor is not at stake. Any supposed threat to God's honor is my way out; it gives me the chance finally to release my accumulated anger.

Say I am unhappy with a work of charity that I generously offered to do for a parish which abuses my generosity. I'm unconsciously angry at the parish, but I may chronically explode in holy fury about the way today's youth engages in parties, romances, and rebellious movements. I can all the while maintain my work for the parish and be hailed as a gentle, generous guy in spite of the abuse that I have to take from parishioners who madden me more each day. I don't dare to confront this abuse which is the real source of my anger. I displace it on young people whom I perceive as totally bad.

Of course, trying to live such a pseudo-spiritual life becomes a mess. Genuine human presence is flagrantly destroyed. All these inappropriate responses to people and situations naturally place a great strain on my interactions with them. Even if I keep my mouth shut, people may sense the anger hidden under my sweet external composure. They may be unable to bear this tension. As it turns out, my relationships with many good people are poisoned and finally broken up.

The true spiritual life in me, either in its completion or its hesitant humble beginning, is represented by Christ, by Mary Magdalene, the repentant tax collector, the good thief. Certain hypocritical pharisees, scribes and high priests symbolize the pseudo-spiritual life in me. Each of us is both: Christ and the pharisee. It is our task to let Christ win out in this perennial struggle in the most intimate recesses of our hearts.

Christ is the source and example of true spiritual life. How mild and gentle He was with public sinners, wayward women, tax collectors, thieves and murderers. How he warned against the pseudo-spirituality of certain high priests and pharisees. He was able to admit and feel his indignation, even with people and places linked with the life of the spirit such as the priests and pharisees, the scribes, the vendors in the temple.

Lord, keep me aware
Of whom I feel angry with
That I may not punish the innocent.
Let no anger grow in me
Like a volcano ready to explode
At the slightest remark.
Before I bring my offer to your altar,
Let me be reconciled in my heart
With my brother who angered me.
Free me from the passion and compulsion
To crusade self-righteously
Against your wandering sheep,
Who lost their way.
Cleanse me from the pseudo-gentleness
Of high priests, pharisees, and vendors in the temple.
Let my anger not turn into self-hate
That I mistake for true humility,
Nor let me use your honor
As a pretense for blasting anger
On my brethren.
Oh Christ, win out
In this battle
Between you and the pharisee,
Dwelling also in my heart.

XVIII

GENTLENESS, ANGER AND DESPONDENCY

The pseudo-gentle person, who suffers from pietistic anxiety, is bound to be despondent. His spiritual outlook is dark and melancholic. Afflicted by bouts of depression, his despondency may become so overwhelming that it completely disables him. Incapacitated and paralyzed by depressive moods, he does not function well in daily life. Joy, vitality and heartfelt interest soon die off in him.

More often the person striving after an impeccable life of gentility suffers a less conspicuous mode of despondency but one that has become lasting. Despondency for him is a life style, an abiding way of feeling and acting, so natural that he has lost awareness of how downhearted he is; he no longer sees that his outlook on life is dismal, solemn, and somber. Having been gloomy for so long he has forgotten what it feels like to be otherwise; it is only when he awakens to the fact that he has been living under a clouded, overcast sky that he sees how somber his mood has been. His negative views color his pious words and appearances. He is a prophet of doom, a religious spoil-sort. Humor that is light and pleasant is foreign to him. Only a cynical, sarcastic, destructive kind of wit may be his.

In certain periods or milieus spirituality may be misunderstood by many as a grim denial of joy, graciousness, and refinement. The cause is often a wide-spread bottling up of anger as being unspiritual and the subsequent emergence of anxiety and self-hate. Such people may band together in gloomy sects or they may stay within their own religion becoming a health hazard to those who venerate their inflexible steadiness.

The presence of such moody and morose believers is even more pernicious when they affect a pompous gentility, making them look impressive and convincing, especially to those who cherish already a cheerless dour disposition as a result of their own inclination to dismiss positive feelings as unworthy of the spiritual life. Prophets of doom become especially dangerous when they occupy positions of religious authority and are clearly men of good will and sincerity, who have no suspicion of their contagious affliction.

The continued despondency of the pseudo-gentle person is constantly fueled by anger that he has turned inwardly upon himself. Sustained gloom presupposes sustained self-depreciation. The compulsively gentle face, the sad willful smile, hide a deep and lasting depression, nourished by steady self-hate. He may mistake his self-hate for humility and spend his hours of prayer haranguing himself about how despicable he is in the eyes of God.

Other victims of perverted gentility, however, have no idea that they spend their precious days in hateful self-depreciation. They live their sad despondent lives without suspecting that the true life of the spirit can become a source of peace and joy from which a gentle life style may flow forth. They have so deeply identified their sour existence with the true life of the spirit that they frown on anyone who shows the real joy of a genuine spirituality.

If they are allowed to function as preachers, spiritual directors, or directors of formation, they may do untold harm to people entrusted to their care. They may turn whole communities of faithful into self-hating collectivities that spread gloom and harshness among the population. In the long run, even the pretense of gentleness may be abandoned. A grim life style is openly fostered as a sign and symbol of predestination. Pseudo-spirituality has won out completely; spirituality has become a neurosis. The absence of any true gentility towards self and others in thought, feeling, and manner may be a warning sign that a religious group is on its way to this perversion.

In other cases the despondency of pseudo-spiritual people may be so safely hidden that it is not obvious to anybody. Self-hate comes to the surface in certain self-destructive ways of living that are not clearly and directly linked to their self-hate.

For example, pseudo-gentle jolly fat people may endanger their health and even their life by compulsive over-eating to the point of revulsion and nausea. They rarely realize that they even devour more than their usual towers of plenty each time their gentleness or jolly out-goingness is in danger of collapsing under the pressure of anger that begins to emerge in them.

The normal spiritual person would not have become hungry but angry; he accepts his anger for what it is, coping with it in light of his growing spiritual view of life and its contingencies. The compulsive jolly eater is not even aware of his anger and deeply concealed depression; it may take months, if ever, to help him see the links between his need to be the jolly delightful Christian and the subsequent denial of his rising anger and their relation to his voracious self-destructive appetite.

The same is true of his opposite, that quasi-ascetical, skinny, dour person without appetite, who perpetually feels guilty about an endless collection of trespasses he never committed—tresspasses against abstractions like humanity, world peace, the third world, all the poor, all possible minorities, and so on.

One type of pseudo-spiritual person turns his self-hate into over-eating; another into starvation. And because the underlying cause is the same, one and the same person may shift from one type of self-destructive behavior to the other.

Perverted anger may lead to sleeplessness. How can one sleep when seething with deeply buried anger?

The anger itself is completely unknown. The victim knows only the agitation that constantly oozes from this accumulated anger like lethal radiation; it keeps him wide awake in the fearful quiet of the night. Sometimes he feels attacked by terrible thoughts, such as visual fantasies of accidents happening to dear people near him. He feels bewildered for these are the same people with whom he is so excessively gentle in daily life. He feels tortured by such frightening images, so totally at odds with his angelic self-image.

It would require much well-guided self-examination before he could understand how small irritations with dear ones in daily life, when immediately denied and buried, can snowball inwardly to unbelievable proportions, giving rise to obsessive images and nightmares of horrible suffering afflicting family and friends.

Looking at the history of religions, this perversion of the spiritual life may partly explain the real tortures thought up by people who prided themselves on their spirituality and were eagerly engaged in witch-hunting and persecution of the unorthodox.

Not all despondent strivers after the life of the spirit suffer from insomnia or nightmares. Some do the opposite. They sleep away a great part of their day, unconsciously trying to escape the pain of their heavy-hearted holy life.

Another symptom pseudo-gentle people may suffer from is a self-destructive preoccupation with past failures and sufferings that cannot be undone. Or they may live in an obsessively anxious anticipation of possible bad things that may happen in the future. They worry endlessly and uselessly. It is another way of punishing themselves unwittingly for their lack of genuine spontaneous gentleness, for their unsolved deep-seated anger and aggression. As long as they are obsessively ruminating about past, present and future happenings over which they have no control, there is no room left to become aware of the anger that threatens to ruin their pseudo-gentility.

Their interminable chains of worry are maintained also to dissipate their accumulated anger. The agitation anger gives rise to is now used up in preoccupation with events far removed from the real causes of the anger that is evoked in them by their daily environment. This rumination may be so obsessive and continuous that they feel as if they are going to pieces. Of course, what they are going to pieces with is anxiously contrived gentility, buried rage, and mounting self-depreciation.

Some pseudo-gentle people accuse themselves in the confessional of bad thoughts they cannot stop. They suffer a compulsion to think about a parent, spouse, superior or child as killed by accident, afflicted by cancer, struck down by stroke or heart attack, forced to meet failure in their lives. They feel terrified and desperate. They do not realize that they are not guilty of such obsessive fantasies. Neither are they aware that they feel anger precisely with the persons to whom they feel obliged to exert constantly saccharine sweetness and love. The bad thoughts may disappear once they are able to really feel the full extent of their pent-up anger—to accept it, express it to some trusted and understanding person, illumine it slowly with the new spiritual vision they are acquiring gradually by developing a true spiritual life. If such thoughts are destructive and frequent, spiritual direction combined with other professional help may be needed to solve the angry problems involved.

Not all fears and their symptoms are as excessive. As we have seen earlier, most of us who strive after the life of the spirit develop parallel with it, and secondary to it, a pseudo-spiritual gentle personality that comes to the fore in times of crisis and stress. At such moments we too will have difficulties with anger that we try to deny. The anger we deny periodically will be neither so intense nor so pervasive as constantly denied anger and anxiety in people whose lives are dominated by pseudo-spirituality.

In these far milder cases we may only be aware of uneasy feelings at certain moments with different people or in certain situations. We do not necessarily need personal spiritual direction or professional help to become more aware of this temporary acting up of our secondary pseudo-spiritual personality. Right reflective reading, meditation, prayer, and instructions by a well prepared spiritual teacher can help us to gain insight, to become easier, freer, more joyful and genuinely gentle people, gentle first of all with ourselves and more faithful to our primary true spirituality.

Lord, rescue us
From despondency,
From an outlook,
Dismal, solemn and somber;
From prophets of doom,
Who grimly denounce
Graciousness and joy;
Moody and morose men
Of dour disposition
Whose contagious affliction
Veils the eyes of many
From your joyful tidings.
Cure them from their self-hate,
Their despondent mood,
The anxious frown on their brow.
Help also those among us
Who under the guise of outgoingness
Hide a heavy heart;
Those who are torn to pieces
By sickly feelings of guilt
For the suffering of all humanity
And cannot believe truly in your Redemption;
Those who lie awake
Night after night
Helplessly exposed
To the lethal radiation
Of deeply buried rage
They do not know;
Those who are bewildered
By images of pain and torture
Destroying dear ones.

Touch their flushed forehead, Lord,
With your healing hand.
Relieve the burden
Of their heavy hearted
Holy life.
Halt the endless worries
That consume them needlessly.
Relieve us, dear Savior,
From the pent-up anger
That spoils
Our precious days.

PART THREE

GENTLE COMMUNION
WITH
DIVINE MYSTERY

XIX

GENTLE LIFE AND DEATH OF DESIRE

It is difficult to be gentle. One reason seems to be that I set my heart anxiously on too many things. I may be hungry for power, desperate for money, desirous of knowledge, status, strength or beauty. I struggle for success and fame and vehemently pursue my individual perfection. There is in such pursuits a hidden violence. I am driven by the idle hope that peace will be mine when my dreams and desires come true. I forget that true fulfillment is a gift of God. Only he can fill me as I desire. Outside of the divine encounter, I can speak about incidental gratifications but not about ultimate fulfillment.

God's presence alone gives full meaning to my existence. Only his Kingdom silences my restlessness. To enter this presence, I must give to my life a new form. Not the form of anxious cravings I have made ultimate, but the form of a graced Christian life, shaped by the one desire that surpasses all others: the desire for the Kingdom. Grace invites me to the only possible fulfillment of human life its engulfment by the Holy. The Holy Spirit inspires me to empty myself like Christ from all other desires: "Your attitude must be Christ s. . .he emptied himself" (Phil. 2:5—7).

When I make my selfish desires ultimate, I may get in return small doses of satisfaction. I should never mistake these for true fulfillment. The moments of satisfaction that do emerge occasionally soon vanish like flowers that delight us with their fragrance only to wither away. What may remain is a memory that makes me feel good and sad at the same time. Sad because the passing gratification of desire proved again not to be the fulfillment I had foolishly expected it to be.

I may lose the gentle life style due to the vehement way I seek gratification in this life. Every time I pursue passing pleasure in the expectation of final fulfillment I find disappointment instead. Disappointment in turn intensifies my impatient striving after momentary gratification. Such anxious striving makes the gentle life impossible. It heightens the vehemence of my life. What keeps me violent, what steals my gentleness, is the furiousness of my pursuit, the desperateness of my clinging to pleasure when it comes, the tension of my struggle to avoid its diminishment, the bitterness of my resentment when it is no longer there Such vehemence is of no avail. Whether I like it or not, pleasure is doomed to fade. The more I set my heart on it as a possible fulfillment of my life, the more I will suffer at its vanishing away.

As long as I put my hope in incidental gratifications, I will remain moody, anxious, unsettled. Equanimity escapes me. One day I am elated, the next down-hearted. My mood varies with the alternation of momentary pleasure and its unavoidable frustration. Satisfying some of my desires may give me ease for a time but this ease cannot last. I feel a letdown whenever I find out what seemed like satisfaction led by no means to the fulfillment of the real me.

A man lived in a poor place where frugal meals were the order of the day. An unexpected inheritance made it possible for him to move. He carefully chose a hotel highly recommended for its outstanding kitchen. He thought about the marvelous meals soon to be savored by him. Used to being hungry, he fancied that all his problems would be solved once he could count daily on well-prepared nourishing food. He moved into the hotel. The meals were excellent indeed. His daily hunger was a thing of the past. The first month he was elated. Then he began to take his culinary affluence for granted. This problem being solved, other problems and desires began to emerge. Each day reminded him anew that he had not yet found final fulfillment.

This man's mistake was not that he looked for adequate daily nourishment. Once he had the means to get it, he made what appeared to be a wise and necessary move. His mistake was to imagine that satisfying his hunger would automatically solve his problems and silence every desire.

The satisfaction of my selfish wishes does not silence them. For a while they may be quiet. Then they return, more insistent than ever, even if they assume another form. The man satisfied his hunger but soon craved other things. So fleeting is the satisfaction of a selfish wish that it begins to fade the moment I achieve what I so anxiously longed for.

As long as my life is filled with impatient desire, I will find neither abiding peace nor gentleness. I will lose the gentle life. Jesus tells me to renounce this anxious life of restless striving after worldly gratifications *as if they were ultimate.* If I respond to this grace of renunciation, He promises me the true life. He calls it a life eternal. Not only will it last forever in the hereafter; it also has an eternal character in this world. This life of desire for the Divine is a sharing in the love and desire of Jesus for His Father and His Kingdom. It is a desire that God's will be done no matter what my own selfish wishes are. Therefore, this life is not ephemeral like the life of selfish desires made ultimate.

The life of desire for the Divine ought to encompass the many other desires that give direction to my life. Wise desires are rooted in my one desire for the Kingdom, in my ultimate concern for union with God. Desires directed to this end mellow and make gentle the human life of striving; they ready me for divine fulfillment.

Desires rooted in selfishness are excessive and excite me needlessly. They imprison me within the cage of a self-centered little life cut off from God mankind, nature, and world. I live in abysmal ignorance about the true meaning of human life and its fulfillment. My understanding is clouded by an accumulation of self-centered desires that come to me from my own imagination and culture, from parents and friends, from TV and other news media. These self-oriented desires fascinate me by their promise of lasting fulfillment via travel, nourishment, knowledge, possession, beauty and fame.

Selfish desires stifle my real possibilities for love and understanding. They make it impossible for me to abide with the Lord or to be gently present to self and others, to the events He allows to be. My life becomes self-centered and narrow. My entire existence is gripped by selfish motives. I seek fulfillment in a never-ending round of fleeting gratifications. The upshot of it is that I develop an all pervading stance of dissatisfaction, worry, restlessness and tension.

The kingdom of selfish desires is nothing like the gentle Kingdom of God. It is not really a kingdom; it is an anarchy of lust, greed, envy and anger. Each new satisfaction increases the violent craving for more and varied gratifications. The reign of the isolated self, seeking its own salvation, is a reign of endless disappointment.

The source of true self-fulfillment and its subsequent peace and equanimity is God alone. The source of disappointment and its subsequent tension and restlessness is the self in isolation from Him. Selfishness defeats itself. It seeks fulfillment through momentary satisfaction but leads only to lasting dissatisfaction.

To find God I must overcome selfish desires. I cannot overcome them by repression or by denying that they are there. Admitting their existence in me, I must allow the Holy Spirit to let me become aware of how futile they are to real fulfillment. Slowly and gently, I must let them die off. "I solemnly assure you, unless the grain of wheat falls in the earth and dies, it remains just a grain of wheat. But if it dies, it produces much fruit" (John 12:24).

If my selfish life of blown up desires falls down and dies, the real life of divine desire may arise and produce the fruit of oneness with God. St. Paul describes this detachment beautifully:

> I tell you brothers, the time is short. From now on those with wives should live as though they had none; those who weep should live as though they were not weeping, and those who rejoice as though they were not rejoicing; buyers should conduct themselves as though they owned nothing, and those who make use of the world as though they were not using it, for the world as we know it is passing away (1 Cor. 7:29–31).

In this attempt to die to selfish desires, I must be careful lest my effort deteriorates into another forceful expression of selfishness. It must not become an ego project, willful and arrogant. Death to self must be approached gently, patiently, trusting in God alone. "Good and upright is the Lord: thus he shows sinners the way. He guides the humble to justice, he teaches the humble his way" (Ps. 25:8–9).

Gentle Life and Death of Desire

A gentle death to the life of selfish desire can only be granted to me when I acknowledge that I am a sinner unable to save myself. Then He will show me the way. He will guide and teach me. He will cover and shield my attempts: "With his pinions the Lord will cover you, and under his wings you shall take refuge; his faithfulness is a buckler and a shield" (Ps. 91:4—5).

Dying to the life of selfish desire, I participate in the saving mystery of Jesus' death and resurrection. "May it (the reception of the Blessed Sacrament) cleanse us from our old selves and bring us into the fellowship of your saving mysteries" (Prayer after Communion, First Sunday of Lent).

Like Abraham, I must not withhold anything: "I know now how devoted you are to God, since you did not withhold from me your own beloved son" (Gen. 22:12). My death to selfish desires in response to His grace will then be precious to my God. "Precious in the eyes of the Lord is the death of his faithful ones" (Ps. 116:15).

SPIRITUALITY AND THE GENTLE LIFE

The man who seeks salvation
Outside you, my Lord,
Will meet with endless disappointment.
Furious pursuit of pleasure
Steals rest and gentleness,
Impatient desire
Prevents abiding peace.
Moments of fulfillment
Vanish like flowers
That delight us with their fragrance
Only to wither away.
How desperately man clings to pleasure,
How vainly he struggles
To avoid its disappearance.
And yet, Lord, we know
That all pleasure is doomed to fade,
To vanish without trace.
So fleeting is
The satisfaction of a wish
That it begins to fade
The moment we achieve
The aim we longed for anxiously.
Desires in tune with the Divine
Mellow and make gentle
This life of striving.
Engulfment by the Holy
Silences restlessness
And frees my soul
From painful craving.
Thus, my Lord, I pray:
Cover me with your pinions,
Hide me under your wing,
Be my buckler and my shield
That I may dare to die to selfish wish:
For the death
Of your faithful one
Is precious in your eyes.

XX

SILENCE AND GENTLENESS

"When peaceful silence compassed everything and the night in its swift course was half spent, down from heavens, from the royal throne leaped your all powerful Word; into the heart of a doomed land the fierce warrior leapt" (Wisdom 18:14—15).

These mysterious words of the Book of Wisdom have been elevated by the Church to the words of the entrance song of her liturgical celebration the first Sunday after Christmas. She applies them to the coming of the Divine Word among us.

In the same spirit, I may apply these words to the coming of the Word into my soul.

I may liken my life to the doomed land into the heart of which the all powerful Word wants to leap. Land is doomed when its springs have dried up, when there is no water from heaven to restore its sources. It becomes parched like a desert; it no longer produces fruit; it produces no flowers, no shadowy trees in which grateful birds nestle and sing, no sparkling streams in which fish can play and multiply—streams that refresh and renew life along their shores.

My life is like this doomed land when the Word is no longer the living Water of my soul, the pure well of my feelings, thoughts, and actions. The living Divine Waters must gather in my heart—the core of my being—before they can begin to renew my life. I should dwell in adoration on that mysterious stream of Divine Love flowing from the Trinity into my heart; then it will swell and swell until it sweeps from the core of my being into all of the parched land of my life; it will become irrestible.

Like a fierce warrior, this divine stream will break through the dikes of my self-centeredness, flooding my spirit, psyche and vital being. Then in and through my transformed life the flood of Divine Love will flow out into the world around me. My life will be like a refreshing stream for all who approach its borders. The doomed land of my life will have been transformed into fertile earth thanks to the miracle of the Divine Flood.

The Word leapt already into my life at Baptism. My participation in the Divine Mysteries, that are the Sacraments, renewed and deepened that Presence.

What I may resist is a fuller presence of the Word in me. My heart may not be truly open to the Divine Flood. The reservoir of my heart may not be filled to the brim with the renewing Divine Waters. They cannot push fiercely over the brim to fertilize all of my existence.

A hindrance to this fullness of Divine Presence is my lack of silence. The Word comes only in a deeper way when peaceful silence compasses everything, when the night is half spent in its swift course.

I may refuse gentleness and silence in my life. I may refuse to enter into the night of inner quiet, of non-resistance to the Divine. Then the Lord will not come to me in a new abundance. My life is doomed to remain parched and lifeless. My land becomes a wasteland.

What is this silence that prepares for the coming of the Lord, Silence can be understood in many ways.

Silence can be experienced as the absence of noise. Silence may also mean the absence of words that are needless, the abstinence of useless talk, the softening of a voice that is shrill and strident.

The cultivation of silence belongs to the gentle style of life. A style permeates what we are and do. We speak about the style of a writer. We mean that elusive undeniable quality that pervades every one of his expressions. We say we know Shakespeare by his style. Similarly, a life style pervades all of our lives.

When we speak about the gentle life style, we speak about something that should reveal itself in all dimensions of our daily living. One dimension of our life is that of our speaking and not speaking. The style of gentility that makes our whole being less resistant to the invasion of the Divine should also affect the important dimension of our life that is our daily speech.

Silence is a gentle rhythm of speaking out and keeping still. When it is time to speak, the virtue of silence leads to a gentle modulation of our words and of the tone in which they are spoken. This silence is the realization of the gentle life style in one area of my life, that of speech.

There is no renowned spiritual master, East or West, who did not praise the gentleness of speech and silence that leaves room for presence to the Presence.

Beyond the silence of speech, however, a deeper kind of stillness is demanded when we strive for a deeper union with the Divine. It is the silence the Book of Wisdom speaks about: the peaceful silence that *compasses everything:* the silence that goes deeper than the gentle modulation and spacing of my spoken words.

I am also to silence the unspoken words of psychic power that dominate my life unwittingly. The words that crowd my awareness, that leave no place for the Word in my soul. Unspoken words that have the harsh, selfish sound of the ego life. Manipulative ambitious words that render the land of my life parched and dry. Anxious, tense and scrupulous words that command me to force myself into moralistic self-perfection.

These powerful unspoken words are far more harmful than the spoken ones. They halt the One Word that wants to fill my life. If I cannot silence these words, they will shape my anxious thoughts, fire my already fiery imagination, inflame my passions, harden my will, give rise to forced postures and angular movements, erupt into aggressive words and actions.

Such actions, postures, movements, passions, thoughts and imaginations reinforce in turn their hidden source, the unspoken words that keep the Word away.

But the Book of Wisdom tells me about a blessed silence that compasses everything; it compasses also unspoken words in my subconsciousness and the harmful thoughts and actions that flow from them.

The silence that compasses everything is not the silence of my spoken word alone. The silence that modulates my speaking and its pauses is only a particular realization of my gentle life style; it operates only in one area of my life, that of the spoken word. The silence that encompasses everything is as wide in scope as the gentle life style itself.

When I silence words that are a source of agitation and manipulation, I can never go far in that attempt alone. Alone I am not powerful enough to escape the driving power of the subconscious keywords I have taken over from a culture obsessed by the drive for status, pleasure, power and possession. Only the all powerful Word, like a stern warrior in the heart of a doomed land, can redeem me from their evil fascination.

I have to leave the daylight of the marketplace of false values and the words that stand for them. I must hide in the benign night wherein all words fall silent and all things soften to shadow. The blessed night which helps me escape my tyrannical ego words, my excessive self-preoccupations, worries, actions. This night may loom up for me as endless. In fact, its course is swift; for this night is not spent in the tiring ambitions, schemes, and worries of the competitive day. Neither do I have to wait till the end of the night to taste its consolation.

As the Book of Wisdom hints, already when the swift course of this night is half spent the all powerful Word will leap down from the royal throne into this heart of the doomed land.

Divine Word
My springs dried up.
Parched is the land of my life like a desert:
No trees in which birds nestle and sing
No streams in which fishes play and multiply.
Without divine waters
My life is a land that is doomed.
You, Divine Word,
In whom I am spoken from eternity,
Through whom I am created in time,
With whom I am elevated, divine;
You alone are the well
That refreshes my being.
I adore the stream of your love
Flowing into me ceaselessly.
Let the stream swell and swell
Till it sweeps
Into the farthest corners of my life.
All-powerful Word, you are a mighty flood,
A fierce warrior breaking through
The dikes of my resistance.
Divine Waters, fill me to the brim.
Let your life in me become
A refreshing stream of love
For all who approach my borders.

Eternal Word, without you
My land is wasteland.
Grant me the silence
That makes me less resistant
To your invasion.
Free me from words that are needless;
Soften my strident voice.
Teach me the gentle rhythm
Of speaking out, of keeping still.
Teach me the modest spacing,
The gentle modulation of spoken words.

Teach me the mystery
Of a silence that compasses everything.
Silence the unspoken selfish words
That dominate my life.
Destroy the inner words
That keep the Word away.
Free me from the fascination
Of the words of people
Obsessed by power, pleasure, and possession.
Hide me
In that blessed night
Wherein all words
Fall silent,
All creatures
Soften to shadows.
Before that night is spent
Let me taste its consolation:
Your Presence, Divine Word,
In my life refreshed and purified.

XXI

GENTLE COMMUNION WITH
DIVINE MYSTERY

". . .learn from me, for I am gentle and humble of heart. Your souls will find rest" (Matt. 11:29).

Jesus asks me to be gentle hearted. Saint Paul, in whom the Lord came alive, was gentle as a mother with his fellow Christians. "While we were among you we were as gentle as any nursing mother fondling her little ones" (1 Thess. 2:7).

Do I gently nurse my own soul, as Saint Paul nursed the soul of his people? Or do I punish my soul in disappointment when it feels wounded and small? How can I find rest for my soul if I talk to it harshly? Do I see the Divine Master of my soul as a master of affliction or a master of gentility?

"I think thoughts of peace, and not of affliction. You shall call upon me and I will hear you; and I will bring back your captivity from all places" (Entrance Song, 31st Sunday).

I may feel that the Eternal thinks thoughts of affliction about me. Perhaps this is because I cast Him in my own image. Say that somebody tricked me. My first thought was to get even with him. I thought only of revenge. Maybe I myself was unjust to another. I felt sure he cast upon me the same thoughts of affliction I would have cast on him, had he done the same thing to me.

Fortunately the Lord's thoughts are far removed from mine:

> The Lord is gracious and merciful
> slow to anger and of great kindness.
> The Lord is good to all and compassionate to all.
> Ps. 145:8-9

His are thoughts of peace, not of affliction. "Peace is my farewell to you, my peace is my gift to you; I do not give it to you as the world gives peace. Do not be distressed or fearful" (Jn. 15:27).

No matter how shaken I am or how badly I carried on, when I call upon Him, He will hear me. He will bring back my captivity from all places. My concerns are so spread out that serenity keeps eluding me. I feel captivated by popular movements, pet projects, fiery ambitions, social involvement. These concerns may drive me on relentlessly. I push people around to make my plan come true and I am pushed around in turn. I drop my prayers to gain time for action. I skip moments of rest and recollection. No longer do I find time to gently nurse my soul. I have put myself into captivity.

Now is the time to call upon the Lord. He will bring back my captivity from all places. He will grace me with gentility. Instead of my tasks captivating me, I shall carry them. He helps me to break their overly busy hold on my life, teaching me how I can maintain myself gently in regard to them. He helps me to still and quiet my soul, to nurse it back to life as gently as a nursing mother.

Arrogance is one main cause of my captivity. I take on more than I can handle. I involve myself in too many things at once. I set goals that are obviously too sublime for me. Rest is mine only when I can truly say:

> O Lord, my heart is not proud
>   nor are my eyes haughty;
> I busy not myself with great things,
>   nor with things too sublime for me.
> Nay, rather, I have stilled and quieted
>   my soul like a weaned child.
> Like a weaned child on its mother's lap,
>   so is my soul within me.
>   Ps. 131:1-3

My need for achievement easily spoils spiritual gentility. Once willfulness takes over my life, it perverts prayer, love, friendship, leisure. I become a stranger to the quiet strength and goodness of a peaceful life lived in the presence of God. How can I be at ease when I base my worth on accomplishment alone? I become too anxious about my perfection. I confuse my performance values with my true value for God. Performance will always be less than perfect. Sooner or later a sense of futility may overwhelm me. That can be a moment of grace. It may teach me to center my life in the Divine Presence from which I steadily emerge. My life may then become less forceful, more gentle.

Gentleness is an important condition for the spiritual life. The life of the spirit emerges and grows in gentility. A gentle life style affects all my ways. It changes my view of myself and others. It makes me work, speak, feel and act in a different manner. It creates an atmosphere truly conducive to worship and surrender.

Gentility becomes possible when I begin to experience my life as more than the doing of practical things, more than the attainment of calculated success. This kind of growth can only happen when I say yes to the divine dimension of human existence. This dimension of divine mystery does not float above my daily doings as something ethereal and unreal. It is found in the midst of activities.

Gentle communion with the divine mystery in which all reality is anchored is the heart of real life. Such communion should be of vital concern to anyone who wants to live his everydayness easefully and effectively.

I cannot live gently as long as I put myself—with my pet ideas and projects—in the center. For then I have already overextended myself. I have already done violence to life as it really is. I may need to develop a forceful life style to keep up my enhanced self-importance and to maintain this delusion for others. Any view that focuses exclusively on self is willful and, for the spiritual life, ultimately absurd.

To become less aggressive, more gentle, I must see the little me within the great landscape of grace and presence within which my short life enfolds. I should not focus exclusively on my worries, desires, interests and difficulties. I may pay attention to them from time to time, as a passerby would, but not for long. An anxious look at the merely immediate blurs everything else in my picture of reality. I miss the bright clearness of the divine plan and presence from which my life emerges at every moment.

My life cannot be lived gently until it rests in that mystery, until it has become that which it is meant to be—one of the countless small channels for the flow of the Divine Will in the universe. The Divine Will is a mighty symphony. Its music is the playful self-expression of the Eternal Father in time and space. Within the Divine Word who became man, my life is called to be a tiny contribution to this symphony.

Assuming this perspective on life keeps me humble and gentle. The more I live in this gentle way, the more I become available to the hidden power of the Divine in my life. I allow it to work on me through circumstances unimagined, in directions unknown and often against my design and desire.

When I live willfully, I easily ignore the divine light in which my small situation is illumined. I am too busy with the pursuit of power in regard to the things I can handle forcefully and cleverly. I do not live gently enough to sense the divine mystery in whom I live and move and have my being.

Such gentleness, far from making me weak, gives me a sure hold upon daily life and its surroundings. The personal and practical things I have to deal with are enriched immensely in scope and meaning. No event excites me unduly or terrifies me beyond recall. Each occurrence can be gently accepted as a small and passing incident lit by the divine light. The grace of a gentle vision brings new coherence to my life, an equanimity not easily to be shattered.

I may have lost my gentility because I have lost this sure hold on the eternal which alone can give my existence meaning, steadfastness, and direction. I must learn with God's grace to move in the omnipresence of the Divine like a fish moves gently and graciously in the water. The end of my spiritual journey reveals the quiet harmony of my spirit with the Infinite Spirit in response to His attraction and gentle nudging. The journey to God happens almost in spite of myself. I am like a tiny iron filing attracted by the magnet of the Divine. A power beyond myself decides the direction of my life.

Living the spiritual life thus implies more receptivity than forcefulness. Pragmatic questions such as "What is best for my personality?" and "What is most useful to society?" are secondary. The first decisive question is a question of daily lived attention to that which tells me what my life should be like in the mysterious plan of God, whether or not this plan calls me to foster the development of some practical aspect of my personality or some current need of society.

The gentle life is a life of easeful efficiency; it is a life that has forgotten its self-centered ends because of its absorption in the mystery of the Divine Will. Spiritual life is never my doing; it consists in my being drawn by God in His own good time where He wants me to be.

My spirit, like the spirit of all men, is an unfinished creation, one on which the Divine Spirit is always at work. The moment God makes me gentle and flexible enough to become aware of this creative action is the moment my real journey begins.

The gentleness that prepares me for the spiritual life is not the same as the gentleness that is a gift of this life. The latter could be called infused gentility. Preparatory gentleness is a gift of God too. He allows me a large role in its acquisition. Preparatory gentility is one fruit of asceticism. It does not have the deep, abiding quality of infused gentility, which is a pure gift of God. The latter overwhelms me. I can only utter a humble yes as it permeates my soul.

Gentility does not come at once. Bit by bit I feel its attraction and a corresponding dissatisfaction with my more aggressive ways. Bit by bit my soul responds; until a moment comes when I realize that my life style has begun to be transformed from vehemence to gentility. Guided by a new light, I cross the frontier between self will and God's Will. When I remain faithful to this way, infused gentility may be given to me. My new but limited gentility may slowly or suddenly give way to an infused divine gentility. The unseen Love has invaded my soul. Its intimate nearness melts the last vestiges of self will and ego violence. He who first incited my seeking begins now to fulfill it.

Gentility became possible because of my willingness to renounce greed and ambition, because of my grateful response to the attraction of unseen Love. The gentle life style may now become the humble correspondence of human gentility with Divine Gentility. My communion with Him may be maintained at the center of my self.

Don't talk harshly to my soul
When I am wounded and small
For you are slow to anger, Lord,
Of kindness to all.
When I cry out in distress
Nurse me back to life
As gently as a nursing mother.
When I ponder things too sublime,
When I put my worth in self-perfection,
In calculation of accomplishment,
Free me from such wilfulness
Through the gentle action of your love.
Holy is my life in your presence, Lord.
In you I rise daily
Like Venus from the sea,
Like Phoenix from the ashes.
You are the landscape of eternity
In which my life unfolds
Like a blade of grass after winter's cold.
The symphony of your Holy Will
Is a playful expression of Eternal compassion
Flooding time and space.
Let me be a note in your symphony,
A tiny iron filing
Drawn to you, Magnet Divine.
Let me move in your presence
As a fish moves gently in water.
Let no event excite me unduly
Or shatter me beyond recall.
Let me live all things as passing incidents
Reflecting your light.

XXII

GENTLENESS AND PLAYFULNESS

Divine gentility
is the secret at the root of a playful life, that shares in
the playfulness of the Eternal Word. As the Book of
Proverbs says:

Yahweh created me when his purpose unfolded,
before the oldest of his works.
. . .
I was by his side, a master craftsman,
delighting him day after day,
ever at play in his presence,
at play everywhere in his world,
delighting to be with the sons of men.
(Prov. 8:22-23;30-31)

Gentleness places playfulness at the heart of our
spiritual life. Playfulness helps us to be fluent and
flexible, to mitigate seriousness, to dull the edge of
anxious alertness.

To gently participate in the playfulness of Divine
Wisdom at the beginning of time, before the world
was made, relieves us from the pressures of sheer
utility. Without playfulness of spirit, we lose the

sense of mystery. We merely take our part in the well ordered troops of busy workers moving to expand the anthill of modern life. As long as we take our work too seriously, we cannot be playful.

Gentle playfulness is lived in those rare moments when I feel at one with the Divine Presence, finely attuned to His inspiration, released from divisive concerns. I feel gracious, with the soft, flowing grace of a dancer, joyous with the lightheartedness of a child. Such moments grant me a glimpse of eternity, a rehearsal of the playful life to come. For a breath-taking moment, I see the divine playfulness lighting up the world of daily appearances. No longer blinded by arrogant sophistication, make believe poses, empty words, I respond to grace with graciousness, blissfully at one with the Eternal Presence that fills the universe.

God was by no means obliged to create, redeem, and unfold this world. All these events evidence the playing of the Eternal in time and space. In that divine play, people, events, and things are called to find their place and meaning in the outpouring of Divine Love that transfigures the cosmos.

My life is a ship on the sea of time, gently moved by an Eternal Wind mysteriously at play everywhere at every moment. The soul thus moved by God's love is like a butterfly flowing with the soft evening breeze in playful flight.

The divine play is gentle. He knows how brittle we are. He plays with infinite gentility because He treasures us infinitely. We are like flowers tended by a careful Gardener, flowers that last but for a moment and then, in full bloom, are transplanted before His countenance.

This Love created me free to share in this play. But I can harden my heart and betray the mysterious play of people, events, and things in which I am inserted from eternity.

I am not only free; I am also fallen. Fallenness bespeaks a vulnerability that often tempts me to isolate myself from the divine game. Because of this fragile condition in which I live, the gentle moments of ease and playfulness may be few and far between, at least in the beginning of my spiritual life. It is the graced gentle life style that prepares for them and helps me to maintain them.

Aware that my fragile life involves peril and tragedy, I may become too grave and serious. The playful component of gentleness is meant to ease its earnest component. For gentleness is not mere playfulness; it is seriousness too—a playful seriousness, a gentle gravity.

I am not gentle about things I cannot take seriously. Gentleness implies respect for the fragile person or thing I cherish. I am, for instance, not serious about dirt or dust in themselves; they do not call forth respectful care in me. Far from treating them gently, I treat them differently. I wrinkle the dust rag and shake out the mop.

What I take seriously, I may be gentle toward. Seriousness belongs to gentleness; it is, however, a seriousness modulated by playfulness. Gentle seriousness is not like the solemn earnestness of people who take themselves too seriously. Unmitigated, even scrupulous, earnestness may signify a spirituality that is false and forced.

The earnestness of gentility saves me from being too frivolous just as its playfulness frees me from a harshness that would freeze my spontaneity. Gentleness implies an easy gaiety of spirit announcing itself in a presence that is playful and spontaenous, gracious and elegant, but always filled with the earnestness of respect.

To help us live the gentle life, the Word was made flesh. The Divine Player mingled with the human. In the liturgy of His Church we celebrate and symbolize this graced new playfulness.

Grace may become so prevalent in my life that I need no longer labor to be mindful of God. Living in a spiritual atmosphere becomes second nature to me. Then I can be truly playful as I live my graced life before His face.

No longer overly distracted by surface appearances, I sense the playing of the Eternal in the universe. All creation becomes for me the treasured playground of the Spirit. I become lighthearted and free, filled with joy. My playfulness flows from that freedom and makes me available to the Spirit, but it is the Spirit Himself Who is the source of my new-found divine gentility.

The joy that playful gentleness brings is not merely the joy of passing consolation. Infused gentleness has permanency because it springs from my inner depths where the Spirit dwells. This new playfulness is more passive than active, more a being played than a playing. It is a silent surrender to the mysterious play of the Spirit Himself. My initiative recedes. His initiative takes over.

I may still be engulfed by daily concerns; my weeks may be filled with numerous tasks. I must travel from place to place, bear the burden of grief, disappointment, misunderstanding, still suffer, fail, sin—and yet, already a divine gentility has made itself felt as the deeper ground of my experiential life. Already I am given the better part of Mary. No longer am I a mere seeker after the playful life. Already I will have found it in surrender to the divine play in my soul.

The Spirit plays in me and in human history. These two plays are interwoven. The Spirit wants to play in me as the me that is entwined with history. I must accept history as it comes to me. I must face it as a challenge, creatively.

God's play in history allows for change and transition, even for changes that are not always for the best. They are all meant as invitations and challenges for the chosen in the great play of salvation.

A good player is both flexible and tenacious. The flow of the game moves him without breaking him. The struggling teams of fellow players and opponents seem to crowd him out, but in the long run he comes through. The ebb and flow of the game may take him forwards and backwards, but he tries his best to keep in line with the signals of the person who coaches him.

The player of gentle spirit neither tenaciously clings to the past nor frantically strikes out toward the future. He makes himself available to the Spirit alone, ready for any signal He might give him. No matter how backward or forward, brilliant or dull, aggressive or defensive, his play may seem, what counts is simply the kind of play God wants him to play. Only the Holy Spirit knows the worth of each player and what any conservative or progressive move may accomplish in the overall mysterious strategy of a game that spans the millenia.

I must take the game seriously but not too seriously. I must never lose sight of its passing nature. I may feel sorrow but not despair when familiar customs disappear in upheavals, when cultural accretions of the faith are shaken off, when arguments polarize the people of God, when dissension reigns supreme. It is all part of the game. I must never succumb to a seriousness that isolates itself from the playful component of gentility. I must avoid a somber gravity that kills spontaneity and light-heartedness of spirit. In short, I must never lose my sense of humor.

Neither should I yearn above all to be relevant, to be spectacular, to make my mark, to set things straight. I should be content to play my small part in the divinely ordained game of history in flexibility, in graciousness, in holy joy before the Eternal.

Eternal Wisdom,
May your playfulness light up for me
In the playground of this world and its history.
Fill me with your playfulness;
Grant me the airy grace of the dancer,
The lightheartedness of the child;
Dull the edge of anxious alertness.
Redeem me from idle poses,
From useless words.
Let me be a ship gently moved
By the Eternal Wind,
A butterfly flowing with you,
Soft evening Breeze,
In playful flight.
You know how brittle I am, how I would perish
If you would not treasure me infinitely.
Grant me the grace of silent surrender:
Let me never cling tenaciously to the past,
Never strike out on my own toward the future.
Let me be moved instead by Your strategy alone
That playfully spans the millenia.

XXIII

THE DIVINE CHILD, THE LAMB OF GOD

On that day, you will say:
I give you thanks, O Lord;
    though you have been angry with me,
    your anger has abated, and you
        have consoled me.
God indeed is my savior;
    I am confident and unafraid.
My strength and courage is the Lord,
    and he has been my savior.
With joy you will draw water
    at the fountain of salvation, and
        say on that day:
Give thanks to the Lord, acclaim his
    name;
  among the nations make known his name;
    among the nations make known his deeds,
  proclaim how exalted is his name.
Sing praises to the Lord for his
        glorious achievement;
    let this be known throughout all
        the earth.
Shout with exultation, O city of Zion,
    for the great in your midst
    Is the Holy One of Israel!

                    (Isaiah 12:1-6)

Outside my window a gray winter sky pushes down on a dreary city. Along the river comes barge after barge, carrying heavy loads of coal. A steady din of traffic rises from the parkway: truck after truck and endless rows of cars, their drivers caught in the strain of a restless changing world. Watching them, I wonder how much I too am caught in the frantic rush for profit and position. To go forward in a relaxed way is wise; to run wildly, self-defeating.

Even a noble quest such as the one for spiritual wholeness, may turn easily into a warlike venture. I regard my flaws not as a part of me to be slowly remolded in the light of my deepest self. My deficiencies strike me as foreign invaders to be shaken off immediately. I am not very kind toward myself. Kindness for others is an overflow of kindness for oneself. How can I be gentle with others if I cannot be gentle with myself?

Gentleness and kindness. These words turn my attention toward Christmas, the celebration of a divine gentleness made visible in a child in a manger.

"O God, you have made this holy night radiant with your own brightness," says the opening prayer of the Midnight Mass.

I draw these words into my weary heart. They touch me. I brighten inwardly in spite of the grayness of the winter sky. The push of the traffic along the river does not disturb me as much as it did before. The Divine Child brings into the night of my life a glimpse of light. He brings me the glad tidings that I can turn this darkness into a holy night. He may not

take away the night I am living in; he may not let me
escape the suffering of my age, but he may give me
the grace to take its darkness graciously upon me. I
may have to carry this night with me wherever I go,
whatever I do. I can curse it, but I can also bear it
with equanimity. I can skip the self-pity and try to do
what I can, accept the reality that I cannot grow
beyond the confusion of this era farther than God
allows. Then He will make this accepted night a night
most holy. He will make it radiant with its own
brightness.

> In the wonder of the incarnation your eternal Word
> has brought to the eyes of faith a new and radiant vision
> of your glory. In him we see our God made visible, and
> so are caught up in love of the God we cannot see.
> (From the Preface of Christmas)

The Eternal turns himself into an infant in a
manger; our fearfulness of God's splendor turns into
loving trust. The birth of Jesus has made visible the
gentleness of God.

> Let this be a sign to you; in a manger you will find an
> infant, wrapped in swaddling clothes. (Luke 2:12)

This same little one, weak and vulnerable in his
cradle, is the One of Whom God eternally says: "In
holy splendor, before the day star, I have begotten
you."(Ps 110:3)

God is born not only in a manger. He is born also
in me. This touching manifestation of His gentility
invades my own humanity. As the Church prays in
the Holy Mass, when water is added to the wine, "By
the mystery of this water and wine may we come to

share in the divinity of Christ who humbled himself to share in our humanity."

The mystery of Bethlehem is the mystery of the restoration of divine gentleness to my life. Gentility is the coming out of the Divine Child in me. The first step to gentleness is the humble awareness that this is a divine gift not to be forced; it depends entirely on the Child of Bethlehem. This Divine Child is the interior master teaching me a gentility that brings rest to my soul. He penetrates my soul with a gift of mildness toward myself that is a sharing in God's mildness for me. This mildness makes light the burden he asks me to bear. No longer need I carry the burden of his counsels in a spirit of self-punishment and concern.

> Come to me all you who are weary and find life burdensome, and I will refresh you. Take my yoke upon your shoulders and learn from me, for I am gentle and humble of heart. Your souls will find rest. For my yoke is easy and my burden light. (Matt. 11:28–30)

The gentility of God is touchingly revealed in the manger. Divine gentleness was not lost, however, when this child grew up. It was the leading theme, not only of the childhood of Jesus but of his whole life. So much so that the image of the gentlest of animals, the lamb, is used to bring home to us what Jesus was really like. In tender reverence the Church calls him Lamb of God.

St. John, the disciple especially loved by Jesus and most near to him, tries to show us what eternity is like:

> The city had no need of sun or moon, for the glory of God gave it light, and its lamp was the Lamb. (Rev. 22:23)

Its light was the Lamb. To live in the spirit of Christmas is to live in the light of the Lamb.

The Lord as Lamb is the light of the city of my life. The surrender of a lamb to its fate shows me what the peaceful yielding of Jesus in me should be like in regard to my response to the mystery of the Divine Will. This image of mildness does not mean that I cannot labor with force, show strength when demanded, strike out when necessary. The life of Jesus manifests not only a yielding to the Will of the Father but also an unyielding force when his message was undermined by opponents. How flashing his anger was when he found the temple of his Father turned into a marketplace.

God became truly man. His humanity called forth the whole range of human emotions, those also of indignation, spirited defense, fearless standing forth. Yet the gentleness of the child, the surrender of the lamb, was the distinctive feature of his life as it should be of mine. Serene yielding should characterize my life as a whole as it did his. I as a total person should make myself at one with Jesus' stand of surrender to the Divine always and everywhere. "Your will be done" should be the first and last word of my life.

In between there may be many other words. Words that are spoken by me not as the eternal person I am before God but as the person I am called to be incidentally and temporarily in successive life situations. I may experience many fierce feelings as a fighter for human rights, as a defender of the interests of my family, as builder of a business of my own. In these roles I cannot always be like a lamb. My words and deeds may have to be angry and forthright, as were some of the words and deeds of Jesus. But I do not turn any of these incidental words into the one sacred word that carries my life as a whole.

"Your will be done" is the final lasting word of surrender at the core of my being; it holds my life in tranquillity. It was the first word of the child in Bethlehem.

". . .on coming into the world Jesus said:. . .a body you have prepared for me;. . .then I said: As is written of me in the book, I have come to do your will, O God." (Hebrews 10:5-7)

Other words, deeds, and feelings bring out my surface self, my self insofar as it deals with daily events, people, and things. Such words show the practical side of my life. These attempts to adaptation and effective organization may not always work out as well as I would wish. I may then feel upset as a surface person, but not unsettled deep down where I live the life of surrender of the child of Bethlehem.

I neither repress nor identify with the feelings, deeds, and words of the surface me. I let them happen insofar as they are necessary for my effective handling of concrete life situations. I allow that surface part of my self to become spontaneously angry, aggressive, strategic, maneuvering, pleading, planning, diplomatic, when effective incarnation in the world of human interaction demands such stands. In the meantime the Light of the Lamb, the Divine Child in the depth of my being, softly pulls me back when I throw myself too much into passing situations, when I fall into the danger of becoming totally identified with any of the partial deeds, thoughts, or feelings of my incarnating self.

The continual yielding to the Divine at the root of my life, the Holy Child in me, moderates my aggressiveness. His presence is the divine force of integration at the source of my living. The wolf in me becomes the guest of the lamb. as Isaiah says:

> Then the wolf shall be a guest of the lamb,
> and the leopard shall lie down with the kid;
> The calf and the young lion shall browse together,
> with a little child to guide them.
> (Isaiah 11:6)

When I reach this inner at-oneness, God may send me on my way in equanimity to bring to others the message of Christmas. "Be on your way, and remember: I am sending you as *lambs* in the midst of wolves (Luke 10:3).

When I allow the Lamb to live in me and to make me at one I will be inscribed in his book.

> Only those should enter whose names are inscribed
> in the book of the living kept by the Lamb.
> (Rev. 22:27)

Sharing the suffering of the Lamb that was slain I will share in his glory.

As my vision continued, I heard the voices of many angels who surrounded the throne and the living creatures and the elders. They were countless in number, thousands and tens of thousands, and they all cried out.

Worthy is the Lamb that was slain
    to receive power and riches,
    wisdom and strength,
        honor and glory and praise. (Rev. 5:11-12)

The Divine Child, the Lamb of God

Lord, make the night of my life radiant
With the brightness of your birth.
Refresh my tired heart
With a new vision of your glory.
Make me share in your divinity,
You who share my humanity.
Be my master. Teach me
How to be mild with self and others,
How to bear lightly my daily burden.
Be the lamp of my life,
O Lamb of God.
Teach me to yield peacefully
To the mystery of Your will.
Grant me the wisdom
To be firm without rigidity,
Forthright without harshness,
Forceful without ferocity,
Fill me with the gentleness of the child,
The meekness of the lamb.
Divine Child in me,
Pull me back
When I become too involved in this age,
Inscribe me in your book.
Let me share in your suffering and your glory.
Let me adore you forever
As the Lamb slain for me and all men,
Alone worthy to receive
Glory, honor, and praise